CHESS
FOR
CHILDREN
STEP BY STEP

CHESS FOR CHILDREN STEP BY STEP

A New, Easy Way to Learn the Game

International Grandmaster William Lombardy and Bette Marshall

Photographs by Bette Marshall
Chess Art by John Schnell

LITTLE, BROWN AND COMPANY

BOSTON   TORONTO

Acknowledgment

I wish to thank my good friend David Singer for his invaluable comments and suggestions in the formation of this work. I also wish to thank my newfound friends Paul (Bobby Fischer's lawyer at Reykjavik) and Bette Marshall. Paul's inspiration, encouragement, and suggestions were boundless and indispensable. Bette, aside from her own contribution to this book, provided her partner in this new adventure the push so vital for a person's success. Quite simply, my deepest appreciation is insufficient!

William Lombardy

FIRST EDITION

T 09/77

Library of Congress Cataloging in Publication Data

Lombardy, William.
  Chess for children, step by step.

  Includes index.
  SUMMARY: Simple games teach beginning players how to move each chess piece and what each can do in a game.
  1. Chess — Juvenile literature. [1. Chess] I. Marshall, Bette, joint author. II. Title.
GV1446.L57   794.1′2   77-23183
ISBN 0-316-53091-3

*Published simultaneously in Canada
by Little, Brown & Company (Canada) Limited*

PRINTED IN THE UNITED STATES OF AMERICA

To John (Jack) W. Collins, the teacher of Grandmasters and World Champions, who made chess a truly happy experience for me and so many others.

To Ethel Collins, who cheerfully endured many hours of chess blitzing.

And most especially, to my loving parents who these many years put up with the clutter of my chess books and who certainly must share in any success I will have attained.

William Lombardy

For my husband, Paul, who taught me how to play chess, and for our children, Bob, Matthew, and Allison.

Bette Marshall

A Word from a Grandmaster

As an International Grandmaster of Chess I am much accustomed to complications over the sixty-four squares of the chessboard. I have therefore attempted to keep the teaching text as simple as possible.

Yet, this book is not the ordinary children's chess book. Here the teaching of the moves of the chess pieces is presented so that a child, and indeed any beginner, who reads these pages, *a few pages at a sitting*, will learn more than just the basic moves of the chessmen. He or she will learn not only how to move a chess piece but also what the piece can do in a game.

I hope you will enjoy this fresh approach to beginning chess. I'm sure the beginner who goes through these pages will grow in interest and enthusiasm for the thinking sport of chess. A lifetime of fun at chess is ahead!

William Lombardy

For Children . . . and Other Beginners

Although this book was written especially for children, many of our adult friends have said, "A chess book for children? Maybe if it's simple enough, I can learn too!" So, if you are a child, would you please share this book with your favorite adult!

Unfortunately, many people think that chess is terribly complicated. They try to learn all the moves at once and are discouraged if they can't play a full game immediately. Nobody would ever sit down at the piano for the first time expecting to be able to play with both hands. You must learn the notes, then practice with each hand before putting it all together.

Anyone can learn to play chess one step at a time. In *Chess for Children* we have created a "mini-game" for each of the pieces that will help you understand what that piece can do. Each mini-game is truly a part of chess and is so much fun, for adults as well as children, that it can be played over and over until you are ready to go on to the next game.

When you have learned, step by step, what each piece can do, not only will it be easy to play with all the pieces; you will be playing better than many of your friends who may know *how* the pieces move . . . but not how to *think* like a chess player.

Of course, the greatest players (who, like William Lombardy, are called *Grandmasters*) will win more games than you or I because they simply play better than the rest of us. That's true of any expert. Many of us can play "Twinkle, Twinkle, Little Star" on the piano or hit a baseball, but very few become concert pianists or play ball in the World Series. You don't have to be an expert to have fun playing the piano, baseball . . . or chess!

Bette Marshall

Chess: A Game of Fun and Wits

Because chess is played between two persons, you do not need a big group to play. All you have to do is find a friend who knows how to play. You'll have fun outsmarting each other! After you have learned to play, you can have fun teaching your friends.

To play chess, you will need a **chess set**. Don't buy a fancy set that uses unusual forms for the pieces. You'll want to tell the difference between one chess piece and another easily. A simple *Staunton pattern* chess set is best.

You will also need the playing field called the **chessboard**. If four Pawns fit snugly on one square of your chessboard, then you have the right chessboard for your chess set.

This book is your first adventure in learning the exciting game of chess. As you use it, *always have your chess set and chessboard ready for action in front of you!*

Learning the rules of the game is not very hard, and learning them from these pages should be plenty of fun. This book will help you become a good chess player, and the better you get, the more fun you will have!

The Chess Set

Every chess set has two armies. One side has the light-colored (White) chessmen. The other side has the dark-colored (Black) chessmen.

All through this book, there will be **picture chessboards**, or diagrams. Here are the chess pieces you will see in those diagrams.

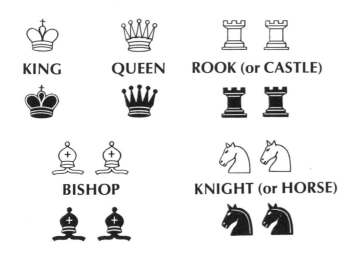

KING   **QUEEN**   **ROOK (or CASTLE)**

BISHOP   **KNIGHT (or HORSE)**

All these chessmen are officers in the chess army, and you as the player are the general in charge. Because each of the pieces moves in a different way, some of them will have more power than others — but you'll learn more about that later.

The lowest man in the chess army is called a *Pawn*. In the chess army the Pawn is the brave, simple foot soldier. But remember that the Pawn is often just as important as the highest officer!

There are eight Pawns in each chess army.

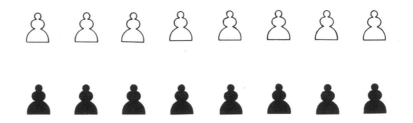

The chess pieces come in a box or bag. But if you want to bring them to life, you must put them on the playing field.

5

The Chessboard

This is a picture chessboard. Before you put a single piece on the chessboard, you must position the board correctly.

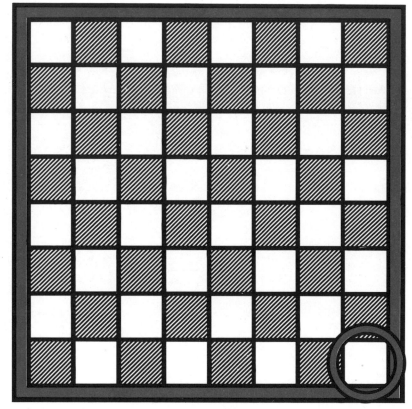

The chessboard is built with little blocks called *squares*. There are sixty-four squares. Half of them are light, the other half dark.

If a *light square* is at your *right-hand corner,* you have the board in the right position. The player on the other side of the board will also have a light square at his right-hand corner!

If you want to have as much fun as possible from playing chess — and win, too! — you should be familiar with every inch of the chessboard. The board is like a road map. If you know the board, your pieces will travel over it that much better!

One look at the chessboard tells you that squares are joined in two ways:

1. They are joined on straight lines.

Some squares stand "shoulder to shoulder" and side by side.

Other squares are joined together by standing one on top of another.

2. They are joined at their corners.

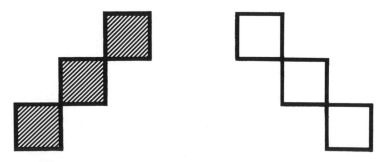

Now you know enough to hear about three new chess words: **rank**, **file**, and **diagonal**.

ABOUT THE RANKS

A line of eight squares standing shoulder to shoulder from left to right (or right to left) is called a *rank*.

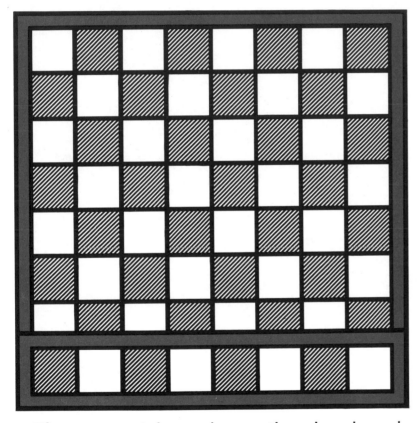

There are eight ranks on the chessboard. Each rank has a number from one to eight. The ranks are numbered starting from White's side of the chessboard.

Rank 1 is marked off in the diagram above. Test yourself by naming the other ranks.

ABOUT THE FILES

A line of eight squares standing one on top of another from your side of the chessboard to your opponent's side is called a *file*.

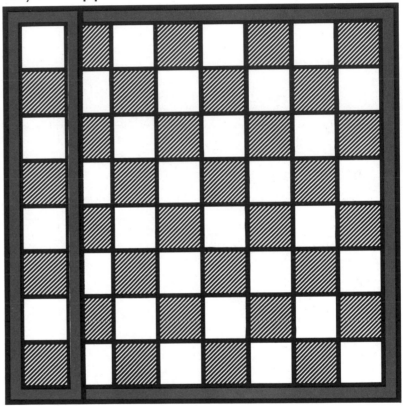

A file is a group of eight up-and-down squares.

There are eight files on the chessboard. Each file has a name according to the letters of the alphabet. From White's left to right (and Black's right to left): a, b, c, d, e, f, g, and h!

The "a" file is marked off in the picture chessboard above. Now you can name the seven other files!

ABOUT THE DIAGONALS

A line of two or more squares joined to each other at the corners is called a *diagonal*.

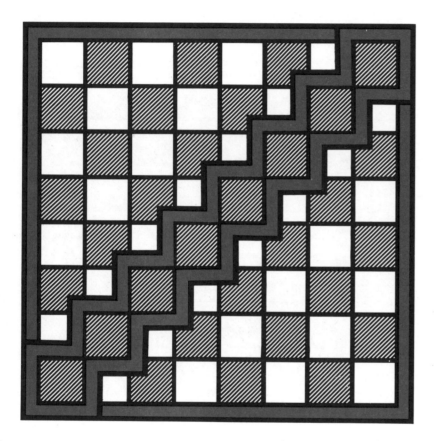

The longest dark diagonal is marked off for you in the picture chessboard above. There are both light and dark diagonals on the chessboard. *The squares in a single diagonal are always of the same color.*

You can easily see that there are many diagonals both long and short on the chessboard.

Because by now you are curious, here is a picture of the chessboard with the two armies set up in full battle lines!

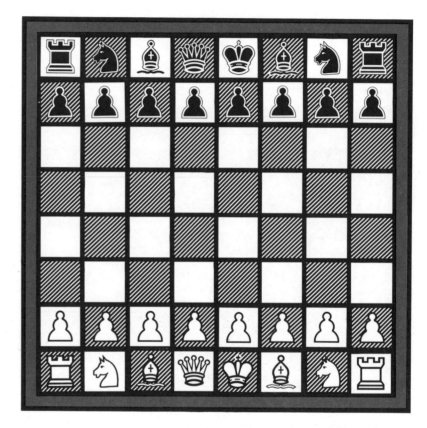

Although you can set out the pieces, you are not ready yet for a full-size game.

First you have to know more about the chessboard. A good general knows every inch of the battlefield. After you have become very familiar with the board, then you will discover the powers of the pieces.

You should already know the name of each piece. For practice, point to each piece and say its name out loud!

Chess Notation:
A Name for Each Square

Ranks and files have names, and so do squares. To really know the chessboard, you'll want to know the name of each square. Learning the names of the squares is very simple.

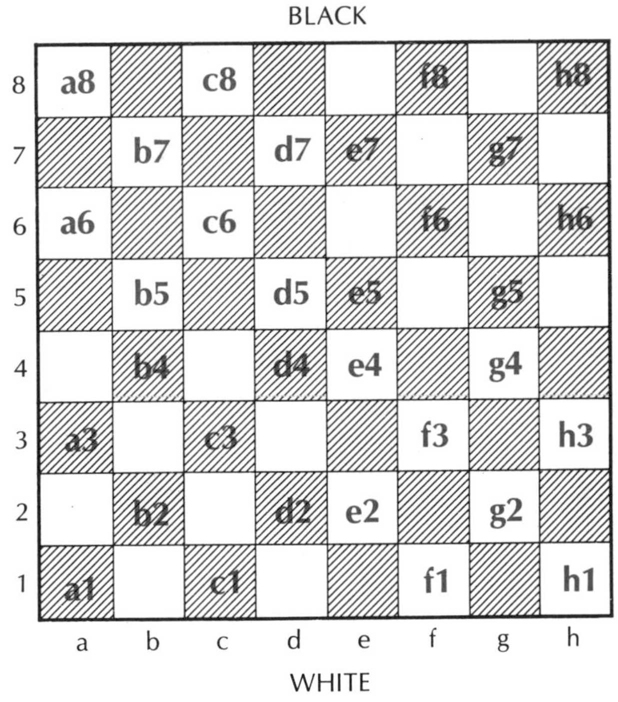

BLACK

8	a8		c8				f8		h8
7		b7		d7	e7		g7	
6	a6		c6			f6		h6
5		b5		d5	e5		g5	
4		b4		d4	e4		g4	
3	a3		c3			f3		h3
2		b2		d2	e2		g2	
1	a1		c1			f1		h1
	a	b	c	d	e	f	g	h

WHITE

A look at the chessboard tells you that *each square sits on a rank and a file at the same time.* A square takes its name from both the rank and the file on which it sits.

The square at White's lower left-hand corner is called *a1.* The next square to the right is called *b1.* Look at the diagram at left. Can you call out the name of each square?

This way of naming the squares is called **algebraic notation**, and is just like the alphabet: ABC's!

9

This Is a Pawn

There are always more simple soldiers than officers in an army. The King has seven officers: a Queen, two Bishops, two Knights (or Horses), and two Rooks (or Castles). But the King also has *eight* faithful Pawns!

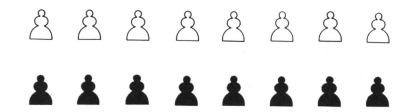

If nothing else, there is strength in numbers. For the number of Pawns on each side is equal to half the army!

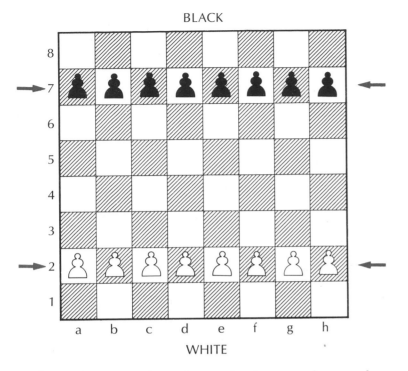

The picture chessboard above shows how the Pawns are set up before the start of both the Pawns Game and the usual full-size chess game.

HOW THE PAWN MOVES

Pawns charge forward one square at a move. In the chess army, the Pawn is the *only* man who *never moves backward*. The Pawn must be brave, for he cannot retreat!

To get the feel of real chess pieces, practice moving the Pawns forward one square at a time on a real chessboard. Try moving both White and Black Pawns. When you play chess, you'll take turns having the White and the Black army. You already know the starting position for the Pawns.

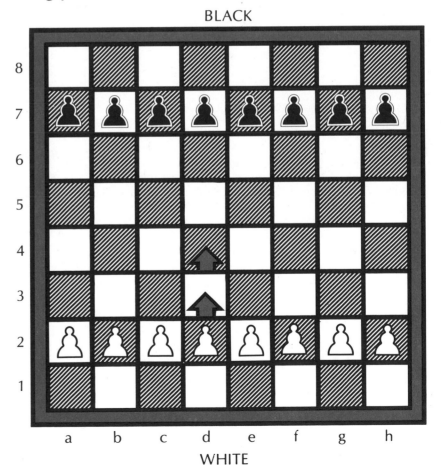

11

HOW THE PAWN TAKES ENEMY MEN

The Pawn attacks at short range. He attacks only *the diagonal squares directly in front of him to the right or left*. If an enemy man lands on a Pawn's **attack square**, the Pawn may take that chessman.

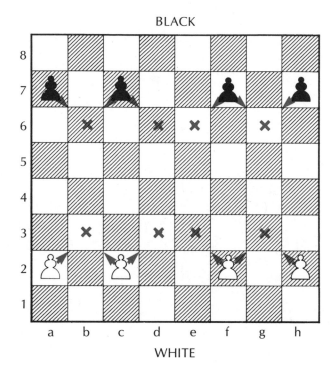

The attack squares of the Pawns in the picture chessboard are marked with an "X." Most Pawns attack two squares. The "a" and "h" Pawns have only half the power because they each attack only one square.

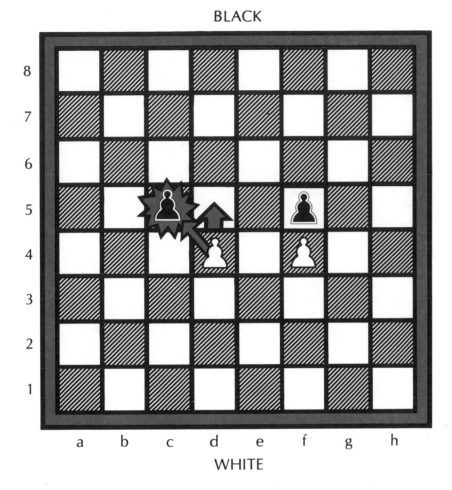

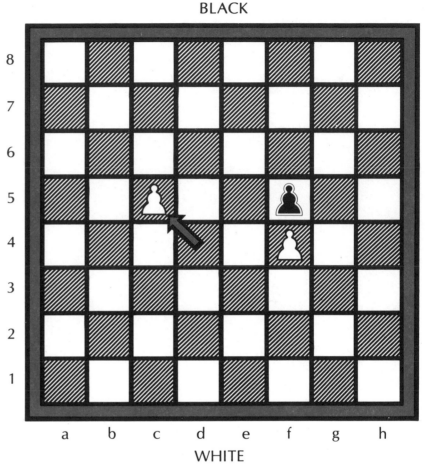

In the picture chessboard above, the "d" and "c" Pawns attack each other! Let's say it's White's turn to move (White is **on move**). If the White Pawn does not want to capture, he can run from danger by moving to the d5 square.

White's Pawn decides to take. The player having White takes the Black "c" Pawn off the board. Then he puts his own "d" Pawn on c5, the square left open by the captured Black Pawn.

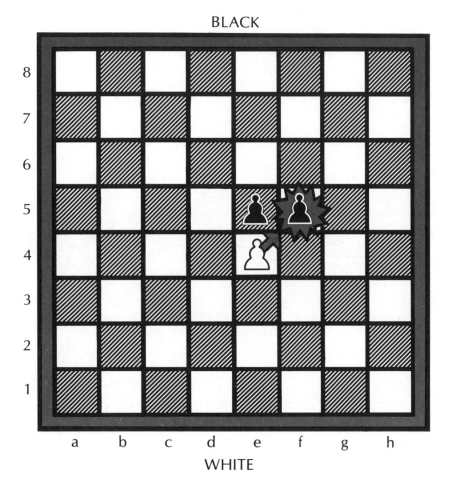

BLACK

WHITE

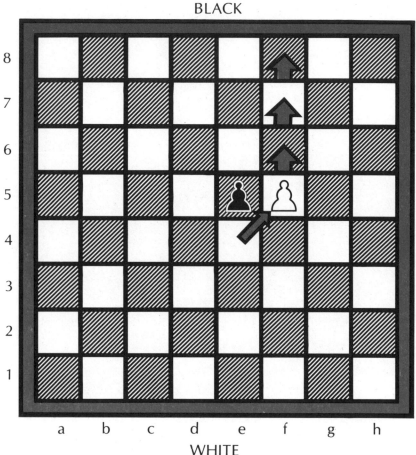

BLACK

WHITE

When a Pawn makes a capture, he always moves his position from one file to another file. After the capture shown above, White's "e" Pawn has suddenly become an "f" Pawn.

Remember: The Pawn moves straight up his home file. But the Pawn *captures* enemy men on a *slant*. The slant is a diagonal square to the right or left in front of the Pawn.

When a Pawn takes an enemy Pawn and another enemy Pawn takes him or one of his fellow Pawns, that's called an even *trade*. One Pawn for one Pawn!

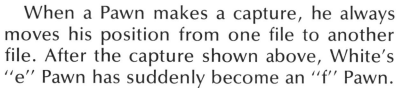

The arrows point from each Pawn to an enemy Pawn attacked. One Pawn attacks an empty square:

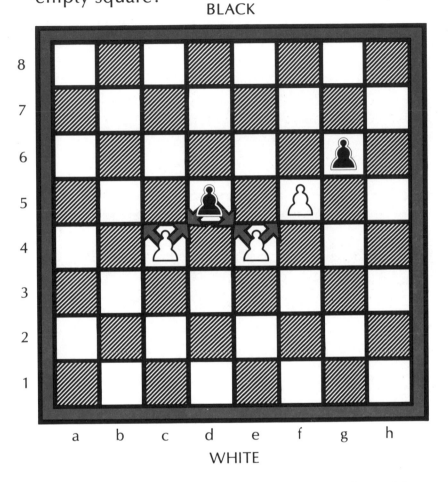

BLACK

WHITE

One piece can never take another piece of the same color. One side in an army never captures its own men!

A helpful hint: If your chessman is attacked by an enemy man,

(1) move the man,
(2) protect it, so that an even trade is possible,
(3) attack another enemy man, or
(4) create a bigger threat than your opponent has. (For example, by attacking a more valuable enemy piece or by threatening the King with check or checkmate. Even the threat to control an important square may balance your opponent's threats! You'll learn more about these ideas later.)

In the picture chessboard above, by taking White's "f" Pawn, Black can trade his "g" Pawn for White's "f" Pawn. White completes the trade. His "e" Pawn protects the "f" Pawn. So the "e" Pawn can take the enemy man that takes the "f" Pawn.

The "e" Pawn looks as if he is attacking his own Pawn on f5. But he is really on defense.

15

Uncovering the Powers of the Pawn

The value of the Pawn is underrated, since the Pawn is the weakest man in the chess army. But the Pawn, the foot soldier in the chess army, has hidden powers that can make him very strong!

PAWN POWER ONE

On its *first* move, each Pawn *may* move *two squares forward*. "May" is the key word. As a chess general, you make the choice for your Pawns. If you think moving the Pawn two squares forward is a bad move, then you don't have to make that move. Move only one square forward — or move another man instead. But remember — if you don't move a Pawn two squares forward on its *first* move, that Pawn may move forward only *one* square at a time for the rest of the game. Of course, you may always move any Pawn not yet moved two squares forward.

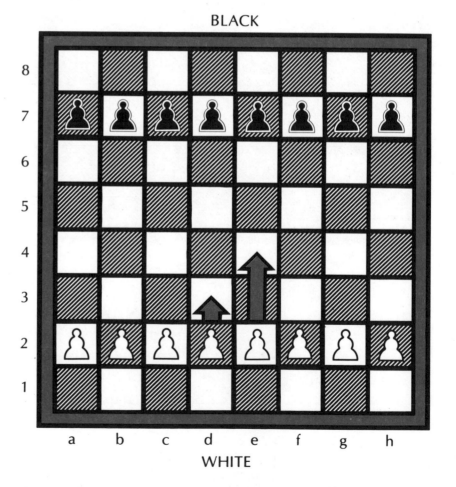

BLACK

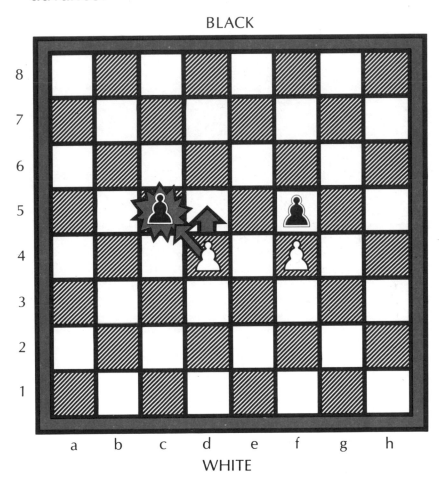

PAWN POWER TWO

Pawns **block** enemy Pawns. When a Pawn blocks an enemy Pawn, neither Pawn can advance.

BLACK

WHITE

White's last move was *Pawn on f2 to f4.* Black blocked with the move *Pawn on f7 to f5.* Both these Pawns are on the same file. They cannot attack each other, so they cannot take each other. Each Pawn blocks the movement of the other.

17

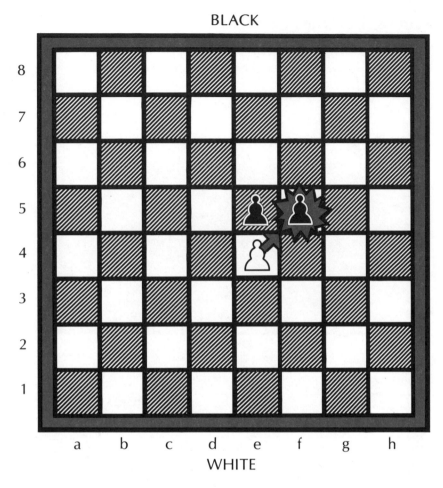

BLACK

WHITE

How to unblock: White escapes the block by taking an enemy Pawn.

PAWN POWER THREE

Pawns connected by their power to attack and defend form a wall. A wall of three or more Pawns is called a **chain**. This is a Pawn chain:

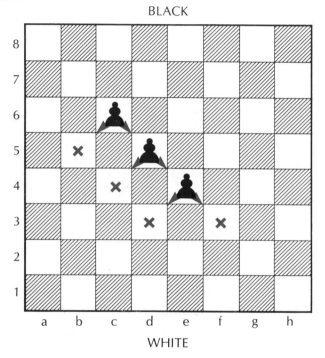

BLACK

WHITE

Remember: Pawns protect members of their own army in the same way they attack enemy soldiers.

In the picture chessboard above, the "c" Pawn attacks the square b5 and defends the d5 Pawn. The "d" Pawn attacks the square c4 and defends the e4 Pawn. Since Pawns do not move backward, the "d" Pawn does not protect the "c" Pawn and the "e" Pawn does not protect the "d" Pawn. The "e" Pawn attacks only the squares d3 and f3.

PAWN POWER FOUR

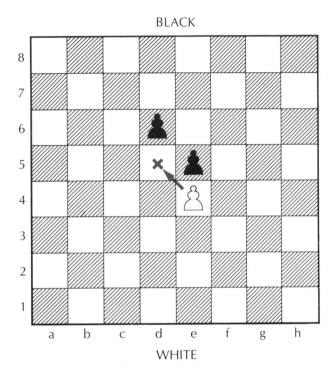

One Pawn can sometimes hold back two or even three enemy Pawns. Above, Black's "d" Pawn cannot move forward without putting itself in danger of capture by White's "e" Pawn.

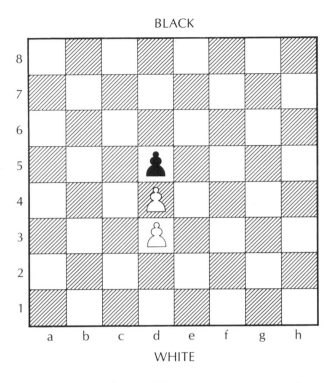

Two White Pawns are on the same file, the "d" file. Two Pawns of the same color standing on the same file are **doubled Pawns**. White has doubled Pawns. All Black needs is one Pawn to block the doubled Pawns.

How do doubled Pawns happen? Simple. You already know that when a Pawn makes a capture he moves from one file to another file.

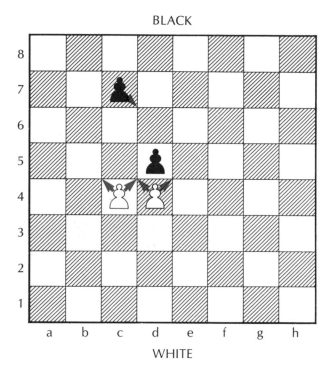

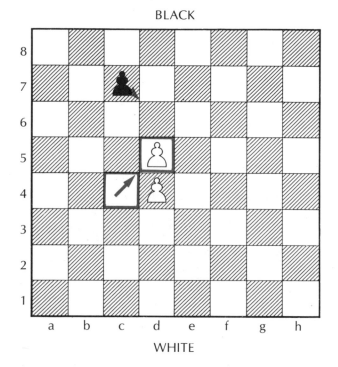

In the picture chessboard, White is ready to take Black's "d" Pawn with his "c" Pawn.

Now White has captured the "d" Pawn and has doubled Pawns. The lone Black Pawn is ready to knock out an enemy advance to d6. So the doubled Pawns are pinned down by only one Black Pawn.

Doubled Pawns are usually bad medicine. There are exceptions, but a beginner should avoid doubled Pawns as far as possible.

The Pawns Game

You now know enough about Pawns to see a sample Pawns Game.

You have read about four Pawn powers. Now you'll see in the sample game how these powers are used. Then you can play the Pawns Game as much as you want!

Later (on pages 66 and 90) you will see two more special Pawn powers. These tricky powers will help you surprise your opponent.

Now let's go on to the rules for the Pawns Game, and then to the sample game.

RULES FOR THE PAWNS GAME

1. Choosing for colors. One player takes a White and a Black Pawn and hides one Pawn in each fist. Then he holds out his closed fists for his opponent to see. His opponent taps a fist, which is then opened. The opponent gets the color of the Pawn in the opened fist. The next game the players switch colors. To be fair, the players change colors every new game.

2. White always has the first move. A player makes one move. Then his opponent moves. First White moves, then Black, then White, and so on, until the game ends.

3. A player may never make two moves in a row. Every move must be answered by the opponent.

4. A player cannot pass. Even if a player has only *bad* moves left, he must play a move.

5. The starting position should be set up as seen below. Note that the Pawns begin the game on ranks 2 and 7, the same positions they have for the start of the full-size chess game.

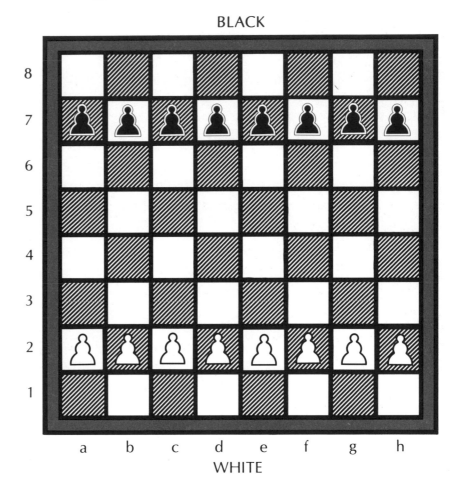

6. If a player moves a piece to a square and takes his or her hand off the piece, then the move is finished. You can't take a move back to play another move. *Think before you move!*

23

HOW THE PAWNS GAME IS WON

7. A player wins the game
   (a) when the opponent gives up, *or*
   (b) by being the first player to take all the opponent's Pawns, *or*
   (c) by being the first player to reach the *last rank* with *one* of his or her pawns!

8. A game is a *draw* (a tie game)
   (a) if the players agree, *or*
   (b) when the player on move has no move left. This is called **stalemate**.

Stalemate happens in the Pawns Game
   (a) when all the Pawns of the player on move are blocked and cannot move forward, *and*
   (b) when the player on move cannot take an enemy man.

(A) and (b) must happen at the same time if stalemate is to be called. Look at the stalemate ideas on page 40.

THE PAWNS READY TO GO!

In the diagram below, you have the Pawns set up as they should be, ready to start play.

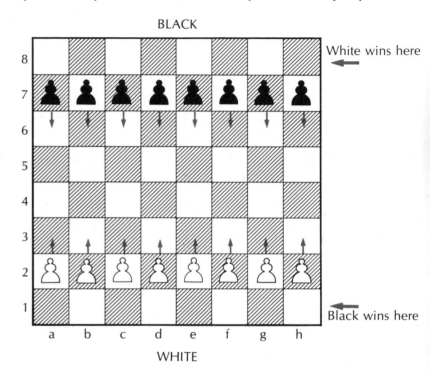

Take out your own chess set and board. Put the Pawns in battle formation, as you see them in the diagram.

Now you are ready to play over the moves given on the sample score sheet.

MOVING PAWNS OVER THE CHESSBOARD

Before the practice Pawns Game, let's review the road map of the chessboard — *algebraic notation*. Then you'll be able to read the moves of the sample game and play them out on your own chessboard.

You have found out the names of the squares of the chessboard, and have named them to yourself, "a1, b1, c1 . . . !" Because you know the names of the squares, you will be able to read a chess move from the score sheet of a game. For now, let's learn to read Pawn moves.

READING PAWN MOVES IS REALLY SIMPLE!

The Pawns of both armies are set up in the starting position on your chessboard.

White's first move on the score sheet (see page 26) reads *f2 — f4*. Which Pawn is going to move? The letter "f" and the number "2" tell you that the Pawn standing on square f2 is going to leave its home square.

The dash (—) after *f2* means *to*. The f2 Pawn is going *to* another square.

Finally, you read the name of the square *to* which the Pawn is going: *f2 — f4*. The Pawn goes to the square f4 on its first move. The full move on the score sheet *f2 — f4* simply means: *The Pawn on the f2 square moves to the f4 square.*

In chess notation, "×" means "takes." For Black's fourth move on the score sheet we do not write: "Pawn on g6 *takes* the Pawn on the square f5." We simply write: "g6 × f5"!

Since White moves first, his moves are shown in the first column. Sometimes a White move is shown like this: 5 e4 × f5 . . .; and a Black move like this: 5 . . . c5 — c4.

An exclamation point (!) shown after a move means *good move*. A question mark (?) means *bad move*.

Now from the score sheet below play out the moves on your own chessboard.

PRACTICE READING PAWN MOVES

	White	Black
1	f2 — f4	c7 — c5
2	e2 — e4	b7 — b5
3	g2 — g4	g7 — g6
4	f4 — f5	g6 × f5
5	e4 × f5	

BLACK

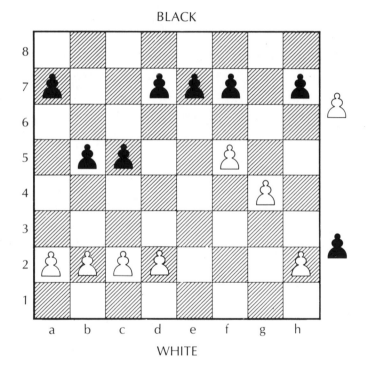

WHITE

If you played over the moves correctly, then you have the position in the picture above on your own chessboard.

If you made a mistake, don't worry. Just set up the Pawns in their starting position and try again!

On his fourth move, Black took White's "f" Pawn off the board and put his own "g" Pawn on the square where the White "f" Pawn stood. Black made a capture!

White also made a capture on his fifth move. He could have made the capture with his "g" Pawn. Instead, he took off Black's f5 Pawn and put his own e4 Pawn on f5.

Now, with the help of the picture chessboards, play out the sample Pawns Game on your own chessboard!

SAMPLE PAWNS GAME

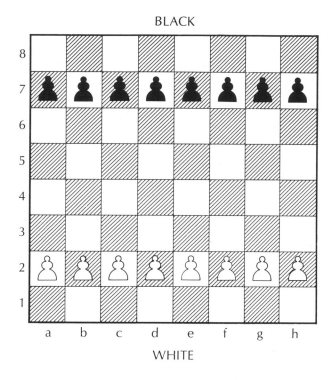

Here you see again the Pawns ready for battle.

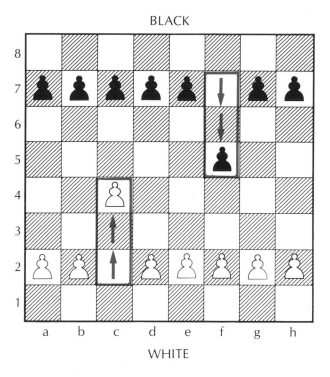

1   c2 — c4   f7 — f5

Both sides march two squares forward. If the players had other plans, they could have moved their Pawns only one square forward.

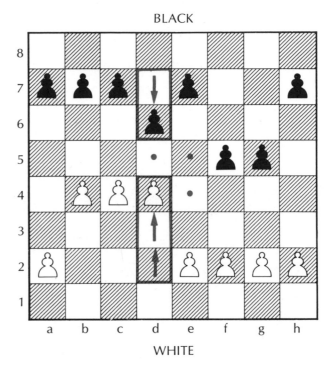

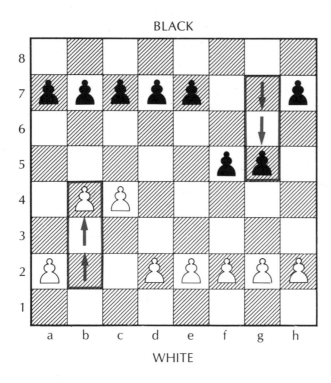

3 d2 — d4 d7 — d6

White finally moves into the *center!* Little by little you will find out why the center is the most important part of the board. For now, just keep that idea in mind.

Black's move prepares to block White's advance!

2 b2 — b4 g7 — g5

White continues action on one side, while Black has his eye on the other side of the board!

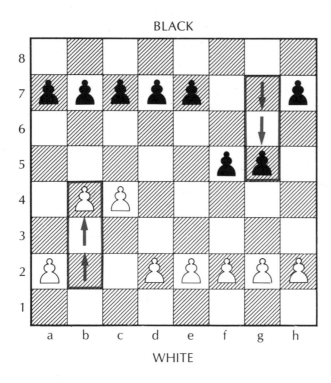

28

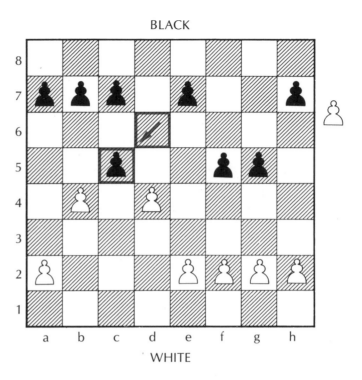

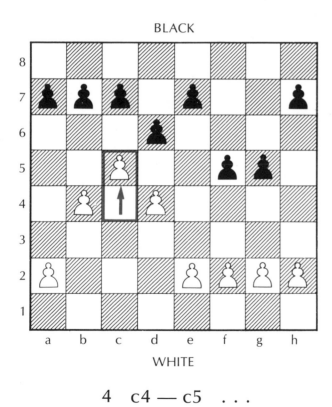

4 c4 — c5 . . .

Driving deep into enemy territory, White's "c" Pawn leaves his comrades far behind.

4 . . . d6 × c5

Black knocks off one invading Pawn. But he also puts his own Pawn in the line of attack of two enemy Pawns!

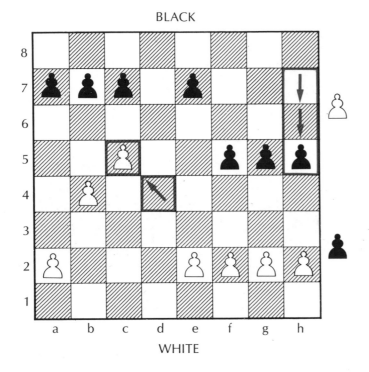

5 d4 × c5 h7 — h5

White replaces his fallen soldier with a Pawn just as dangerous!

Black hurries a counterattack on the other *wing* (side of the board).

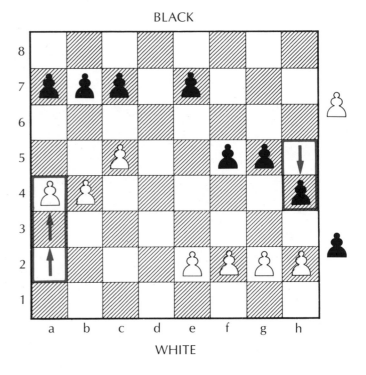

6 a2 — a4 h5 — h4

Pawns that have not yet moved may move two squares forward on their first move.

White takes advantage of this rule.

Black moves his Pawn only one square forward (his "h" Pawn already moved two squares on its first move).

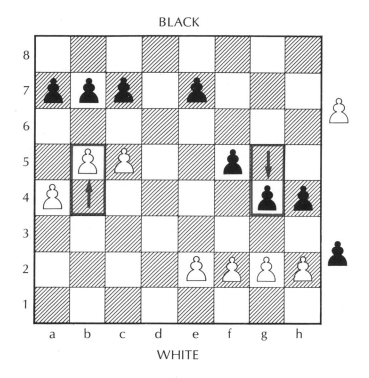

BLACK

WHITE

7   b4 — b5   g5 — g4

Both sides race for the bottom rank on opposite wings of the board!

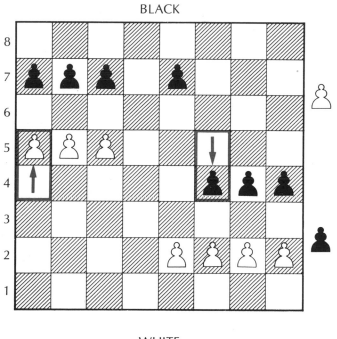

BLACK

WHITE

8   a4 — a5   f5 — f4

At distant ends of the board, both sides have reached a similar position.

The player on move gets the first chance to break through!

31

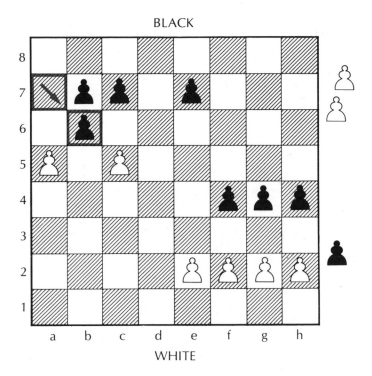

9 ... a7 × b6
Black hopes to save himself by
even trades.

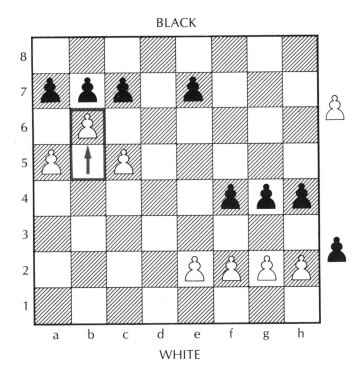

9 b5 — b6 ...
White cracks the middle of
Black's Pawn line!

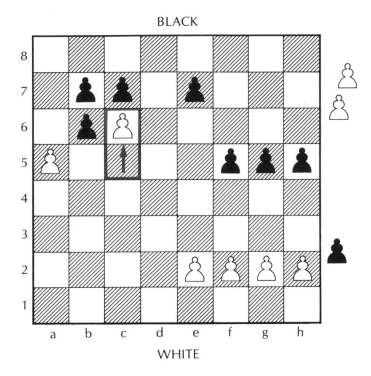

10 c5 — c6 . . .

It costs White another Pawn to force a breakthrough, but *break-through to the last rank is the object of the game!*

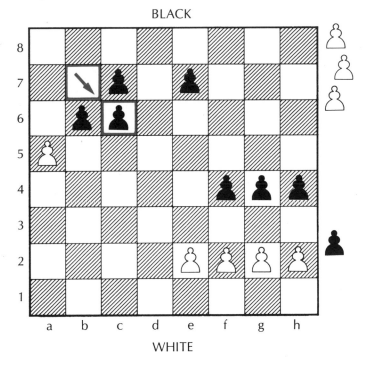

10 . . . b7 × c6

Black cannot force the fight on the other side. Instead, Black must stop to capture, or else White will take Black's Pawn on b7.

33

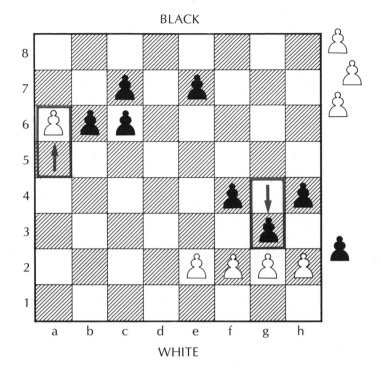

11 a5 — a6   g4 — g3

White's "a" Pawn marches forward with nothing to stop him.

Black's Pawns on the other side enter the race at last! But too late!

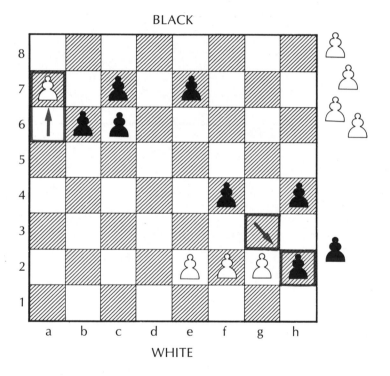

12 a6 — a7   g3 × h2

Each player has moved a Pawn to his opponent's second rank (White in rank 7, Black in rank 2). Only one square to go! But White moves first! Very sad — for Black!

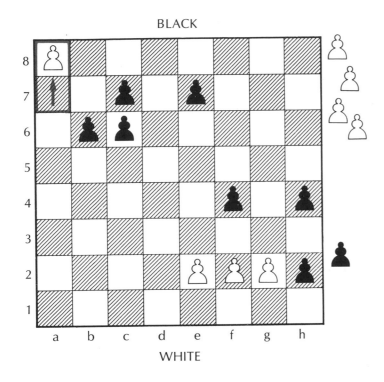

BLACK

WHITE

13 a7 — a8 . . .
White wins the game! Although it cost him four Pawns, he reached the last rank first!

A reminder: Don't pay any attention to the captured pieces off the chessboard. Counting the pieces off the board will only confuse you. The only pieces that really count are on the board! White lost four pieces, Black only one. White still won the game!
Now play the Pawns Game with a friend!

HELPFUL HINTS FOR THE CLEVER PAWNS GAME PLAYER

The positions in the picture chessboards below will help you find little tricks to win the Pawns Game. These same tricks will help you win full-size chess games later on!

Remember: Don't get the idea from the examples that White always wins or even wins most of the time. If you play over the different situations using Black for White and White for Black, you will see that the moves are important, not the color of the pieces.

ONE

BLACK

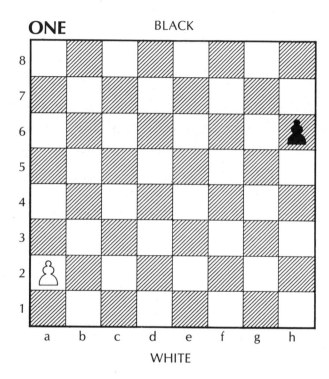

WHITE

Question: Which side has the advantage?

Answer: Whoever is on move gets to the last rank first!

Example:

1	a2 — a4	h6 — h5
2	a4 — a5	h5 — h4
3	a5 — a6	h4 — h3
4	a6 — a7	h3 — h2
5	a7 — a8	The end!

TWO

BLACK

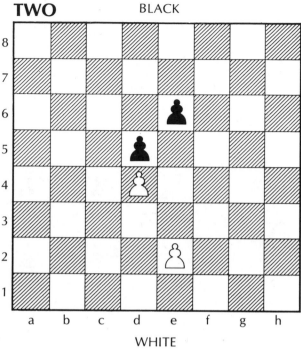

WHITE

WHITE TO MOVE

White has an "extra" move because he has not yet had to move his "e" Pawn from its home base. White patiently plays a waiting move on his first turn. Then Black is forced to give up both his Pawns.

1	e2 — e3!	e6 — e5
2	d4 × e5	d5 — d4
3	e3 × d4	White wins all the marbles!

Compare this example with number nine on page 40.

THREE

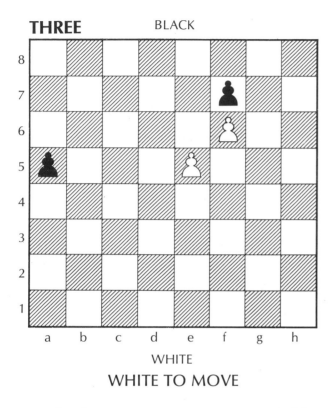

WHITE

WHITE TO MOVE

Black's Pawn can move quickly down the "a" file. And it looks as if his other Pawn pins down both White's Pawns. But White wins, because he is far closer to the last rank.

1 e5 — e6   f7 × e6
2 f6 — f7   a5 — a4
3 f7 — f8   White's Pawn is
             in the goal!

Suppose Black has the first move. Does White still win?

FOUR

BLACK

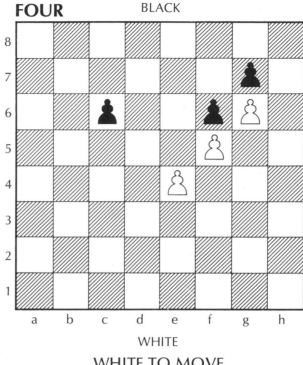

WHITE

WHITE TO MOVE

Black's "c" Pawn is ready to march home. His two other Pawns hold White's three. But White wins by giving up two Pawns. Then his "g" Pawn marches home!

1 e4 — e5   f6 × e5
2 f5 — f6   g7 × f6
3 g6 — g7   e5 — e4
4 g7 — g8!   White's Pawn
             is home!

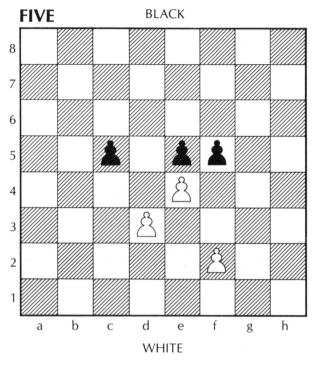

FIVE

BLACK TO MOVE

By a simple trade, Black forces the "d" Pawn out of the way of his own "c" Pawn.

| 1 | . . . | f5 × e4 |
| 2 | d3 × e4 | c5 — c4 |

— and Black's "c" Pawn gets to the last rank long before any White Pawn!

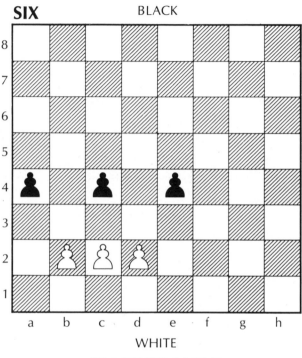

SIX

BLACK TO MOVE

White's Pawns are united. Black's Pawns are broken up. But Black wins, because (a) his Pawns are closer to his last rank, and (b) he can break White's Pawn line by giving up a Pawn.

| 1 | . . . | c4 — c3 |
| 2 | b2 × c3 | a4 — a3 |

— and the Black Pawn speeds home!

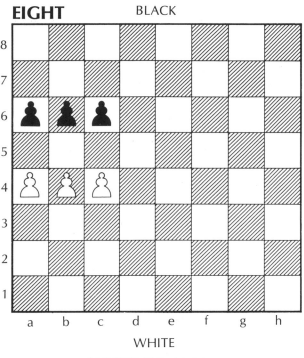

SEVEN

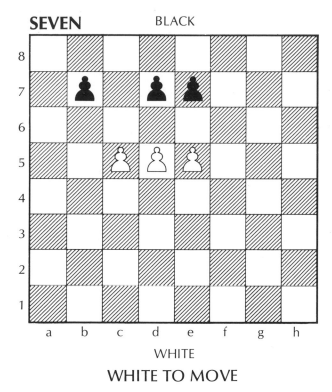

WHITE TO MOVE

This time White's Pawns are closer to the last rank. So he breaks in.

1 e5 — e6   d7 × e6
2 d5 — d6   e7 × d6
3 c5 × d6   And White's
             lone Pawn
             wins the
             game!

WHITE TO MOVE

Everything looks even. But again White's Pawns are nearer the goal. No matter what Black does, White will have one Pawn to reach the end zone!

Example one:
1 b4 — b5   c6 × b5
2 a4 — a5   b6 × a5
3 c4 — c5!

Example two:
1 b4 — b5   a6 × b5
2 c4 — c5   b6 × c5
3 a4 — a5!

In both examples, a White Pawn reaches the goal first!

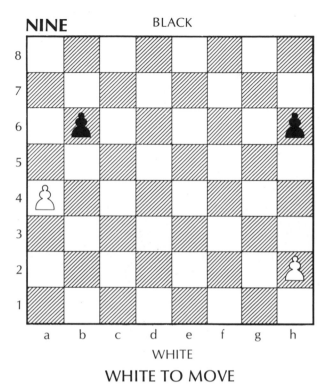

NINE

BLACK

WHITE

WHITE TO MOVE

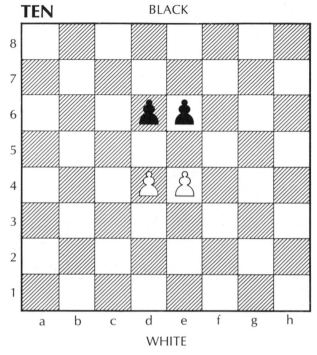

TEN

BLACK

WHITE

EITHER SIDE TO MOVE

Time is important! White has not moved his "h" Pawn. That means he can move it one *or* two squares forward on its first move.

    1 h2 — h3!

By *not* moving two squares forward, White runs Black out of moves!

    1 ...   h6 — h5
    2 h3 — h4   b6 — b5
    3 a4 — a5!

White gets to the goal first! He did not take Black's Pawn because then Black would not have had any moves. The game would have been a draw by stalemate.

The game is a draw because the Pawns will be blocked. Neither side will be able to make a legal move! Both sides will be stalemated!

  (a) White to move:
    1 e4 — e5   d6 — d5
             or
    1 e4 — e5   d6 × e5
    2 d4 × e5

  (b) Test yourself by working out "Black to move."

40

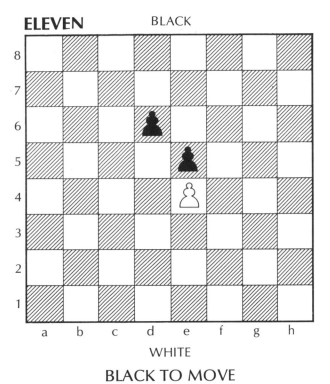

ELEVEN

BLACK TO MOVE

One White Pawn holds down two Black Pawns. Black must move. He must give up a Pawn.

1 . . .   d6 — d5
2 e4 × d5

White wins the race for the last rank! Test the moves on your own board to be sure!

This Is a Rook

In a full-size chess game, and in the Rooks and Pawns Game, each side has two Rooks.

The Rook is sometimes called a Castle — and it does look like a castle.

Many years ago, when a king wanted safety he built a strong castle for himself. From the walls of his castle, he could fight off his enemies. When the time was right, he could also spring fiercely to the attack! This tells us something about the chess Rook. The Rook is a very powerful officer in the chess army. The Rook is stronger than any other chessman except the Queen.

On an open chessboard (cleared of all or almost all other chessmen), the Rook is as strong as an elephant and as swift as a leopard!

HOW THE ROOK MOVES

The Rook rumbles along ranks and files. The Rook *never* moves along a diagonal!

In chess, what is a **line**? A *line* is a group of connected squares. As you already know, the three chess lines are the ranks, files, and diagonals.

What is an **open line**? A line is open when (1) no pieces stand on any of its squares, *or* (2) an attacking piece stands on a line not blocked by friendly chessmen. An enemy piece or even a square may be the object of attack.

In the diagram at right, the Rook stands in the center of the board on completely open lines.

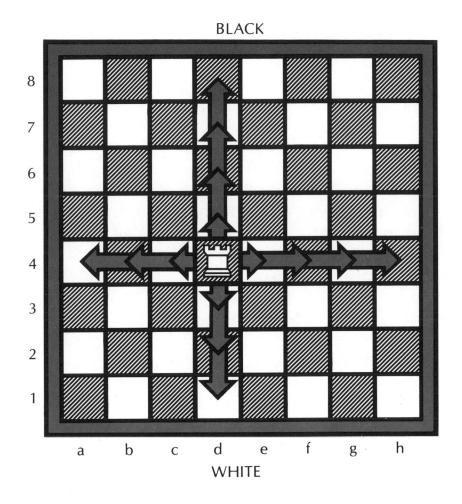

A helpful hint to remember: From the center of the board, every piece has greater power!

The Rook moves forward, backward, and sideways along ranks and files! The Rook does not hop over any piece, friend or foe! In the picture chessboard above, the Rook stands on two open lines. On any one turn of play, that Rook may move to any of the squares where an arrow stops.

43

HOW THE ROOK TAKES ENEMY MEN

The Rook stands in the center of the board. He attacks two enemy Pawns and defends a friendly Pawn. In those directions of attack and defense the Rook lines are not completely open.

If the Rook wants to move to e8, he must first spend a move taking the Pawn on e7! If the Rook wants to move to h4, he must spend a move to take the Pawn on g4.

The e7 Pawn cannot escape the attack of the Rook. The Rook also attacks the "g" Pawn from the side. But by moving forward, the "g" Pawn can escape the Rook's attack for the time being!

Suppose the Rook wants to move to e1? He cannot capture a friendly man. So a straight move to e1 is blocked! He must spend three moves to get to e1. For example, he might first capture the Pawn on g4. Then, after Black's move, the Rook might move from g4 to g1. Finally, again after Black moves, the Rook may move from g1 to e1!

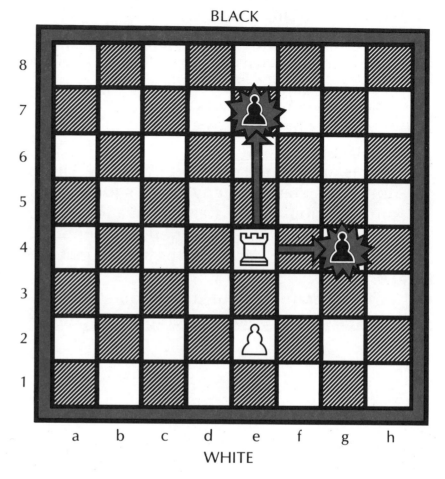

Note that the White Rook captured on his first move. He took the enemy "g" Pawn off the board and put his Rook on the square left open by the captured Pawn.

In the example at right, Black's Pawn is free to move forward. A protecting Black Rook stands behind the Pawn and helps it move forward safely.

A White chessman had better block the Pawn before it gets too far!

If a Pawn is free to move forward without an enemy Pawn blocking the way or able to capture it, that *free-moving Pawn* is called a **passed Pawn**.

Helpful hint: Passed Pawns must be pushed! Keep your eyes peeled for trouble (enemy ambush!) as you push the Pawn to the last rank!

Another hint: Rooks belong *behind* passed Pawns. This is true for an enemy Pawn, which is easier to attack from behind. And it is true for a friendly Pawn. The Rook with its protecting powers helps the Pawn in its forward drive.

Black's Rook attacks White's Pawn!

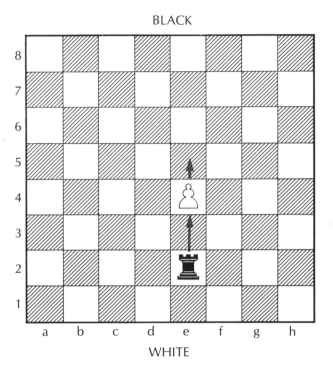

The Pawn can run, but it cannot escape the long reach of the Rook!

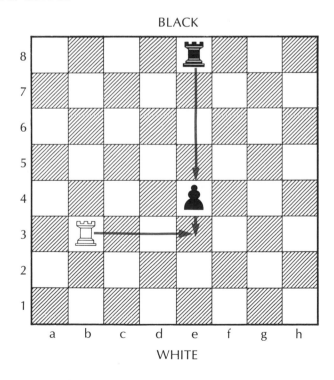

Black's Pawn attacks White's Rook!

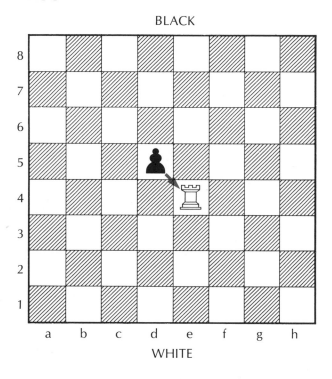

The Rook had better move away, since it cannot attack on the diagonal.

The Rooks and Pawns Game

The Rooks and Pawns should be set up in the positions they would have in an actual full-size chess game (see below). You already know the positions of the Pawns, and it's easy to remember that the Rooks begin by standing one in each corner of the board.

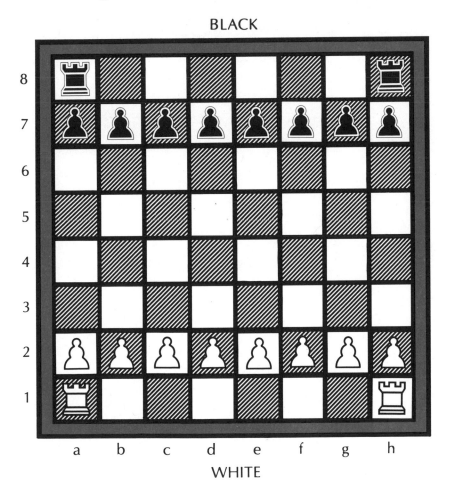

BLACK

WHITE

The other rules for this game are the same as those for the Pawns Game on page 23, numbers 1 to 4 and 6 to 8, with one addition:

If upon reaching the last rank a Pawn can immediately be captured, that's not reaching the last rank! A Pawn must reach the last rank *safely* in order to win the game.

For the attacking Rook, the opposing Pawn home row (rank) is the most important.

The Pawns move very slowly. It takes a long time before many of them have left their starting positions. *An attacking Rook takes advantage of the situation.* The Rook moves to the opposing home row as soon as possible to attack the helpless enemy Pawns!

Note: For reading a game in algebraic notation, the symbol *R* means *Rook*.

> **Example:** *Ra1 — d1* means *the Rook on the a1 square moves to the d1 square.*
> *Rd1 x d4* means *the Rook on the d1 square captures the enemy man on the d4 square.*

Before you play a real Rooks and Pawns Game, sharpen your skill by playing over the sample game below on your own chessboard.

	White	Black
1	e2 — e4	e7 — e5
2	Ra1 — d1	b7 — b6
3	d2 — d4	e5 × d4
4	Rd1 × d4	d7 — d6
5	Rh1 — e1	Ra8 — d8

(see the diagram)

The White Rooks try to break through the middle of the board!

BLACK

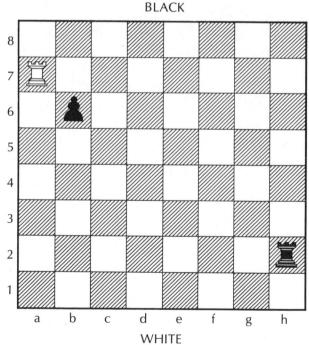

WHITE

	White	Black
6	e4 — e5	d6 × e5
7	Rd4 × d8	Rh8 × d8
8	Re1 × e5	Rd8 — d2
9	Re5 — e7	Rd2 × c2
10	Re7 × f7	Rc2 × b2

(see the diagram)

White's seventh move began a *trade* of Rooks. If White had first played *7 Re1 x e5* (instead of *7 Rd4 × d8*), Black would have responded with *7 . . . Rd8 x d4* — winning a Rook for nothing!

In the picture chessboard, the Rooks are in a Pawn-eating contest. Each side has a Rook on his opponent's home Pawn row!

BLACK

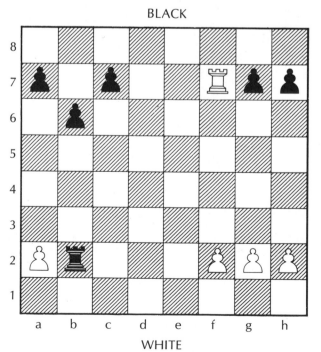

WHITE

	White	Black
11	Rf7 × g7	Rb2 × a2
12	Rg7 × h7	Ra2 × f2
13	Rh7 × c7	Rf2 × g2
14	Rc7 × a7	Rg2 × h2

(see the diagram of the final position of the game)

Black won the game by taking all White's Pawns!

Now you're ready to play the Rooks and Pawns Game on your own.

BLACK

WHITE

48

This Is a Bishop

In the days of kings, queens, and castles, there was always a bishop at the royal court. The bishop served as chaplain to the royal family, and he also advised the king on all sorts of matters. In fact, the bishop often fought in battle alongside his king. And that fighting quality of the bishop is seen in the chess game!

HOW THE BISHOP MOVES

A Bishop patrols the diagonals only! In a full-size chess game, and in the Bishops and Pawns Game, each player has two Bishops.

One Bishop in the army travels on the light-squared diagonals. The other travels on the dark-squared diagonals. A Bishop never moves from a light diagonal to a dark diagonal, or from a dark to a light diagonal. *Bishops stay on their starting color for the rest of the game!*

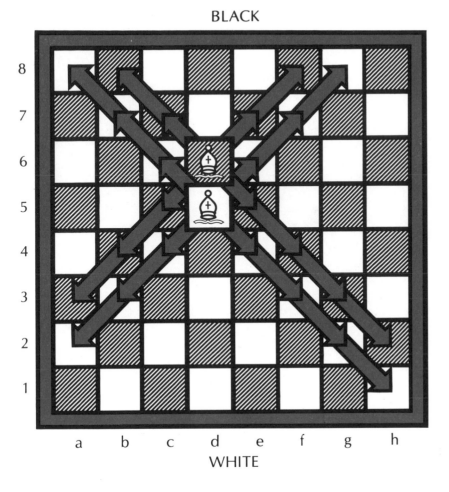

BLACK

WHITE

In the picture chessboard above, there are two White Bishops. One stands on a light square, the other on a dark square. A Bishop makes one move to any square along his color-assigned diagonal (to any square where an arrow stops!).

When a Bishop moves to a new square, he will attack different diagonals. The nearer the center the Bishop stands, the more squares he attacks.

Which of the Bishops in the picture chessboard is nearer the center? The Bishop on d5. He attacks more squares than the other Bishop. Compare by counting!

HOW THE BISHOP TAKES ENEMY MEN

The White Bishop in the picture chessboard below may take either of two enemy Pawns. The Bishop decides to take the Pawn at g7. The player with White simply takes the g7 Pawn off the board and puts his Bishop on g7.

The Pawn at a3 is out of the Bishop's range of attack, but since the Bishop attacks the a1 square, the Black Pawn cannot safely reach the last row!

The picture chessboard also shows how a Bishop and a Pawn work to protect each other. But the d2 Pawn does block the Bishop's movement. The Pawn must move, if the Bishop wants to move to e1 — for no chess piece can take a friendly man, and *a Bishop cannot hop over any piece, friend or foe!*

BLACK

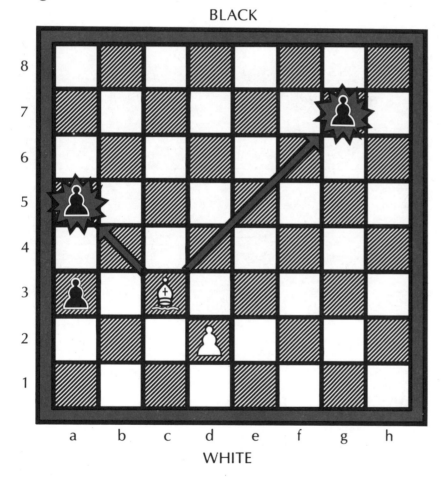

WHITE

The Bishops and Pawns Game

BLACK

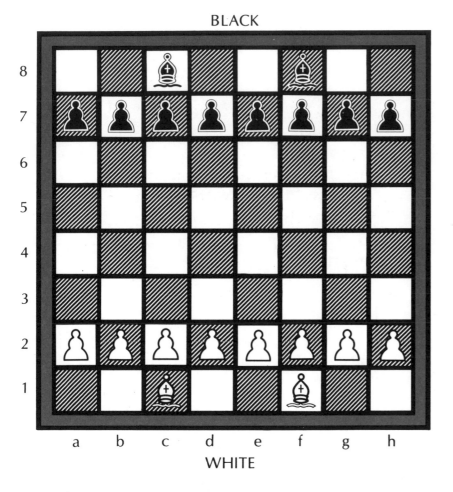

WHITE

The Bishops and Pawns should be set up in the positions they would have in a full-size chess game (see above). Note that the Bishops begin on squares c1 and f1 (White), c8 and f8 (Black). The other rules for this game are the same as those for the Pawns Game on page 23, numbers 1 to 4 and 6 to 8. But re-member: A Pawn must reach the last rank *safely* in order to win the game.

In the Rooks and Pawns Game, you started moving Rooks. Now you'll have good practice moving Bishops.

Note: For reading a game in algebraic notation, the symbol *B* means *Bishop*.

Example: *Bf1 — c4* means *the Bishop on the f1 square moves to the c4 square.*

Bc1 x f4 means *the Bishop on the c1 square takes an enemy man on the f4 square.*

Before you play the Bishops and Pawns Game, sharpen your skill by playing over the sample game below on your own chessboard.

	White	*Black*
1	e2 — e4	e7 — e5
2	Bf1 — c4	f7 — f6
3	d2 — d3	Bf8 — c5
4	f2 — f4	e5 × f4
5	Bc1 × f4	d7 — d6
6	c2 — c3	Bc8 — d7

(see the diagram)

White is ready for a Pawn push in the center, attacking one of Black's Bishops!

BLACK

WHITE

	White	*Black*
7	d3 — d4	Bc5 — b6
8	Bc4 — d5	Bd7 — c6
9	Bd5 × c6	b7 × c6
10	b2 — b4	c6 — c5
11	b4 × c5	d6 × c5
12	d4 — d5	Bb6 — a5

(see the diagram)

It would be better for Black on his twelfth move to play 12 . . . c5 — c4, giving the Bishop breathing room right away!

BLACK

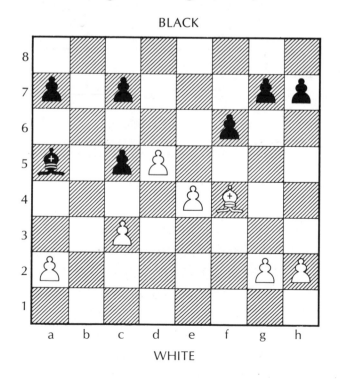

WHITE

	White	*Black*
13	c3 — c4	g7 — g6
14	Bf4 — e3	Ba5 — b6
15	Be3 — d2	f6 — f5
16	e4 × f5	g6 × f5
17	a2 — a4	a7 — a5
18	Bd2 — f4	h7 — h5

(see the diagram)

With only one Bishop left in the army, it is usually a mistake to put friendly Pawns on the same color squares as the Bishop. Doing this blocks the Bishop's movement!

Also, the enemy Bishop working on the same color squares can more easily attack the Pawns!

	White	*Black*
19	h2 — h4	Bb6 — a7
20	Bf4 × c7	f5 — f4
21	d5 — d6	f4 — f3
22	d6 — d7	f3 × g2
23	d7 — d8	

(see the diagram of the final position of the game)

White won, for White's Pawn was the *first* to *safely* reach the last rank! Black's "g" Pawn was only one move away. But one move away is enough to lose!

Now you're ready to play the Bishops and Pawns Game on your own.

BLACK

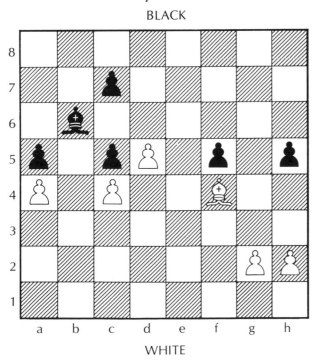

WHITE

BLACK

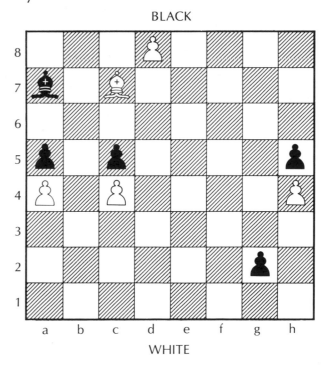

WHITE

55

This Is a Knight

In a full-size chess game, and in the Knights and Pawns Game, each player has two Knights.

HOW THE KNIGHT MOVES

The Knight in shining armor is the King's horseman. His move imitates the action of a horse! The power of the Knight allows him to move like no other chessman. Just as a horse jumps over fences, so *the Knight can leap over other chessmen, both friend and foe.*

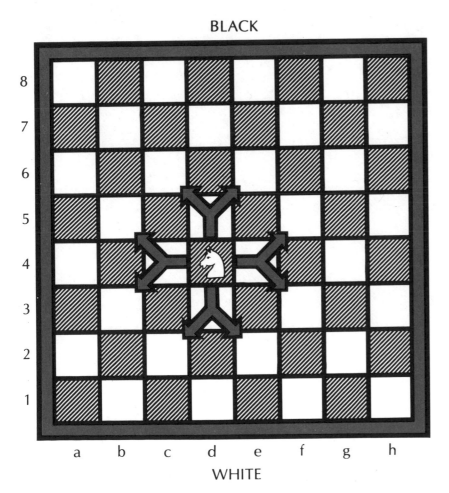

BLACK

WHITE

A single Knight move is made in two steps:
(1) The Knight moves, in any direction, a single square on a rank or file; then,
(2) still moving away from the square where it stood, the Knight moves one square on the diagonal.

You can see in the diagram at left that *the length of the Knight's move is always the same.*

Long-range power makes the Bishop a little stronger than the Knight. But the Knight's tricky jumping power makes him very strong too!

Problem: Put a Knight on different squares on your own chessboard, and practice Knight moves from those squares.

Something to watch: If a Knight begins his move on a dark square, he will end it on a light square, and if he begins it on a light square, he will end on a dark square!

A Knight stuck in a corner is far worse off than any other chessman. Standing in the center, the Knight can attack more squares.

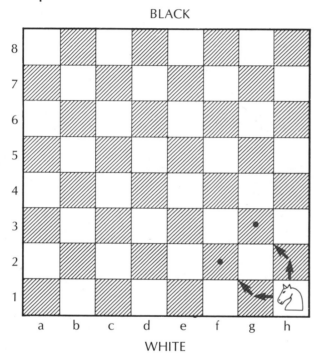

BLACK

WHITE

In the corner, the Knight is hemmed in. He can move to only two squares.

HOW THE KNIGHT TAKES ENEMY MEN

The Knight captures enemy pieces *on any square where it may land!*

BLACK

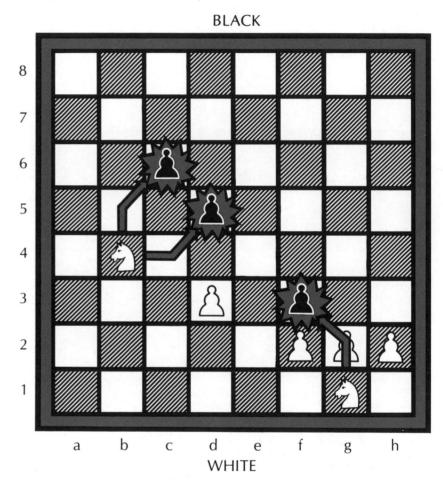

WHITE

In the picture chessboard above, the Knight on b4 can take either the d5 or the c6 Pawn. But if he takes the d5 Pawn, the c6 Pawn can take him in turn! To take the Pawn on c6, a player simply takes the c6 Pawn off the board and puts the b4 Knight on c6, the square left open by the captured Pawn.

The b4 Knight might like to move to d3. But a friendly Pawn is living there! So the Knight cannot move to d3 until the Pawn has moved forward or until an enemy piece captures on d3.

The Knight hops into battle! The Knight on g1 can take the enemy Pawn on f3. The Pawns in front of the Knight do not block him, since the Knight does not have to stop on the squares where the White Pawns sit.

If a White Pawn sat on f3, the Knight could not move to f3. The Knight would be blocked from moving to f3! He could go to either e2 or h3.

The Knight in the picture chessboard below is about to capture Black's *d5* Pawn.

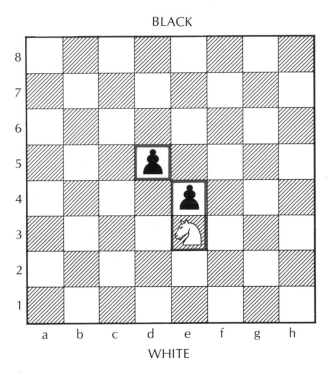

To take the *d5* Pawn, the Knight must pass over the Pawn on e4. On the way to taking the Pawn on d5, the Knight *does not also capture* the e4 Pawn!

The Knights and Pawns Game

The Knights and Pawns should be set up in the positions they would have in a full-size chess game (see below). Note that the Knights begin on squares b1 and g1 (White) b8 and g8 (Black). The other rules for this game are the same as those for the Pawns Game on page 23, numbers 1 to 4 and 6 to 8. But remember: A Pawn must reach the last rank *safely* in order to win the game.

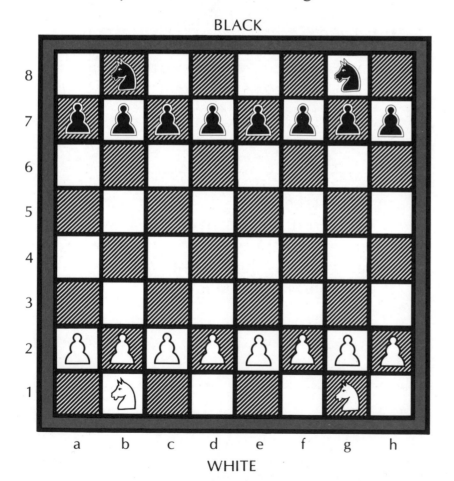

BLACK

WHITE

It's fun to hop around with Horses. This game will give you practice moving the Knights.

Note: For reading a game in algebraic notation, the symbol *N* (the second letter in his name!) stands for *Knight*. (In some books, the symbol *Kt* is used for *Knight*.)

Example: *Ng1 — f3* means *the Knight on the g1 square moves to the f3 square.*

Nb8 x c6 means *the Knight on the b8 square captures an enemy man on the c6 square.*

Before playing a Knights and Pawns Game, sharpen your skill by playing over the sample game at right on your own chessboard.

	White	Black
1	Ng1 — f3	a7 — a5
2	Nf3 — d4	c7 — c5
3	Nd4 — b3	e7 — e5
4	Nb3 × a5	g7 — g5
5	Na5 × b7	Nb8 — c6
6	Nb7 × c5	Nc6 — d4

(see the diagram)

Knights are strong attacking pieces. White has brought one of his Knights into action very quickly!

Speed is indeed important for a Knight! It takes longer for a Knight to reach the opposite end of the board than for a Rook or Bishop.

	White	Black
7	Nc5 × d7	Nd4 × e2
8	Nd7 × e5	Ne2 — f4
9	Ne5 × f7	Nf4 × g2
10	Nf7 × g5	h7 — h6
11	Ng5 — f7	h6 — h5
12	Nb1 — c3	Ng8 — f6

(see the diagram)

Black should have quickly hopped into the battle with both his Horses. Instead, his Pawn moves made a capture chain for the enemy Knight.

Black could have moved his Pawns when they were attacked!

	White	Black
13	Nc3 — e2	Nf6 — d5
14	Ne2 — g3	h5 — h4
15	Ng3 — f5	h4 — h3
16	Nf7 — g5	Ng2 — f4
17	Ng5 × h3	

(see the diagram of the final position of the game)

The game is over! White won because he captured all Black's Pawns!

Now you're ready to play the Knights and Pawns Game on your own.

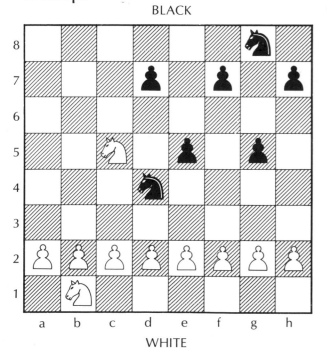

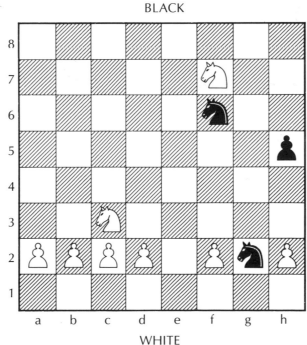

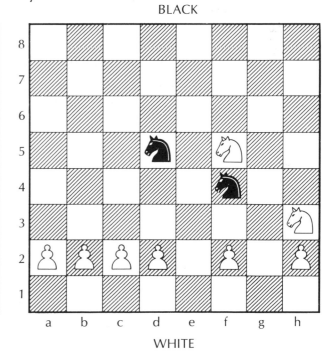

This Is the Queen

The Queen is the King's prime minister. As the King's chief adviser, the Queen has great power, and in the beginning of a game she stands with the king in the place of honor in the middle of the chess army. Since the Queen is so strong, she is able to fight better than any other piece!

A Queen standing on a dark square has the power of a Rook and a dark-squared Bishop. Standing on a light square, she has the power of a Rook and a light-squared Bishop!

You already know how the Rooks and Bishops move. So learning how to move the Queen will be easy!

In a full-size chess game, and in the Queen and Pawns Game, each player has only one Queen.

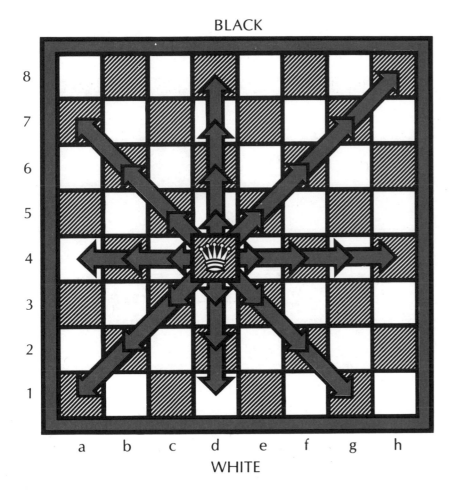

BLACK

8 7 6 5 4 3 2 1

a b c d e f g h

WHITE

THE QUEEN PATROLS RANKS, FILES, AND DIAGONALS

The Queen moves in *any* direction the full length of the board or as far as other pieces on the board will allow.

The Queen looks down *at least one* rank, file, and diagonal at the same time. There is no jumping to the Queen's move, but she is the most powerful and dangerous fighter in the chess army.

From the d4 square in the picture chessboard at left, she may on any single move go to any square where an arrow stops.

The Queen standing in the center on an "open" board attacks almost half the squares on the whole board!

63

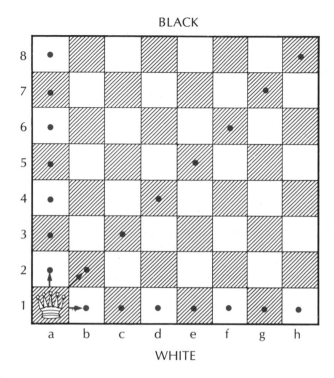

Even from the corner of the board the Queen still can attack more squares than any other piece standing on any square can attack.

Review: The Queen moves to any square on the rank, file, or diagonal on which she stands. Moving from one square and stopping on another completes one move.

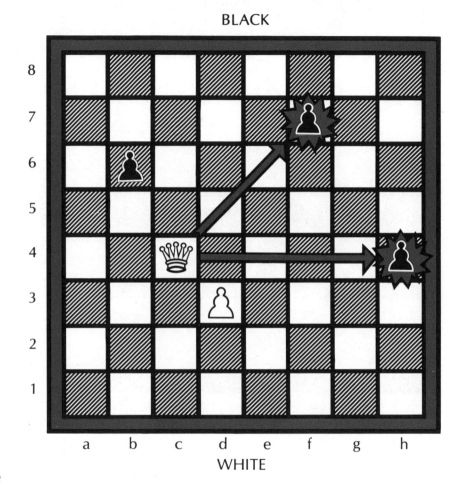

In the diagram above, the Queen attacks two enemy Pawns. She uses her powers of Bishop to attack the Pawn on f7. She uses her powers of Rook to attack the Pawn on h4.

Her Highness should take the h4 Pawn, because that advanced Pawn is more dangerous. It is closer to the last rank. A player simply takes the h4 Pawn off the board and puts the Queen on h4, the square left open by the captured Pawn.

Notice how the White Pawn and Queen protect each other. And although nothing protects the Black Pawn on b6, nothing attacks it either! If the Pawn moved to b5, attacking the Queen, the Queen could capture it!

The Pawn on d3 blocks the Queen's travel and fire power. If the Queen wishes to move to f1, the Pawn must first move up one step to d4. When the Pawn moves to d4, it blocks the Queen's power on another line.

Special Pawn Power Number One

Before we play the Queen and Pawns Game, we must learn a new Pawn power. This power is called **promotion** and is easy to understand.

The starting position of the Pawns is always the same as in the picture chessboard below.

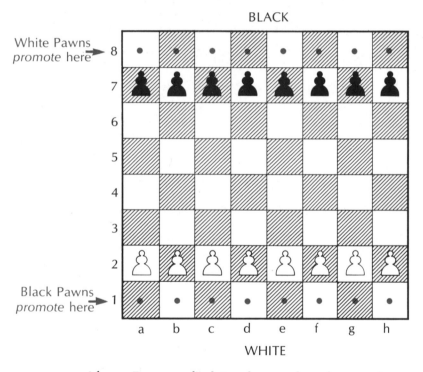

If a Pawn fights bravely through to any square on the last row behind enemy lines, he is rewarded. He is immediately *promoted* to an officer in his army. A player can promote his successful Pawn to a Bishop, Knight, Rook, or Queen. (A Pawn is *never* promoted to a King!)

Because the Queen is the strongest and most valuable piece, a player should *almost always promote his Pawn to Queen.*

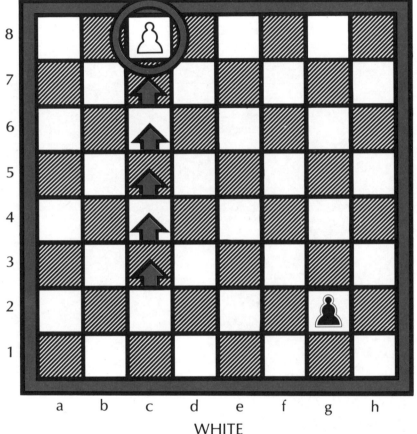

A player begins a full-size game with only one Queen. But the player also begins with *eight Pawns!* If a player reaches the Queening (promotion) rank with all eight Pawns, he can promote all eight to Queen! This means a player can have as many as nine Queens on the board at the same time (the eight promoted Pawns and the Queen he started with)!

In the preceding diagram, the White "c" Pawn has moved step by step to the promotion rank. When the player with the white pieces puts his Pawn on the promotion square, he says, "Queen!" (unless he prefers a Rook, Bishop, or Knight!). He takes the promoted Pawn off the board and replaces it with a new Queen of the same color as the Pawn.

A chess set has only one Queen for each army. But during a game a player might have more than one Queen on the board. If a Rook the same color as the promoted Pawn has been taken off the board, a player can use an upside-down Rook to stand for the new Queen. If a player still has both Rooks on the board in a full-size game, he can use a button, coin, or even a checker to stand for the new Queen.

The moment a lucky Pawn becomes a Queen, that new Queen can make her

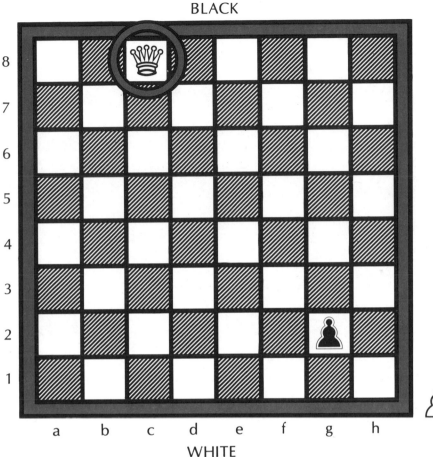

power felt! In the diagram above, the Queen cannot move until Black has taken his turn. But with a new Queen on the board, players should keep their eyes open for new threats.

Notice too in the illustration above that Black's "g" Pawn is about to enter the promotion rank. The player with Black does the same thing as the player with White did.

The Queen is very strong! That is why it is so important for you to rush your Pawns to the promotion rank!

The Queen and Pawns Game

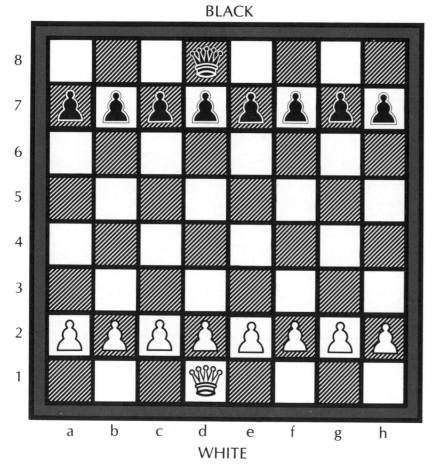

a   b   c   d   e   f   g   h

WHITE

you make a new Queen, you win the game (unless your new Queen can immediately be captured)! You can still win also by taking all your opponent's Pawns.

Playing this game will help you explore the power of the Queen.

Note: For reading a game in algebraic notation, the symbol Q means *Queen.*

Example: *Qd1 — h5* means *the Queen, coming from the d1 square, moves to the h5 square.*

Qd8 x d2 means *the Queen, coming from the d8 square, takes an enemy man on the d2 square.*

Before you play a Queen and Pawns Game, sharpen your skill by playing over the sample game below on your own chessboard.

Set up the Pawns and Queens on the chessboard as if for a full-size game (see above). Note that the Queens begin on squares d1 (White) and d8 (Black) — the White Queen on a light square and the Black Queen on a dark square. Then review rules 1 to 4 and 6 to 8 on page 23. Add to these rules the Pawn promotion privilege. When

	White	Black
1	e2 — e3	e7 — e5
2	Qd1 — f3	f7 — f6
3	Qf3 × b7	d7 — d5
4	Qb7 × a7	Qd8 — d6
5	a2 — a4	Qd6 — b4

(see the diagram)

When you play the full-size chess game, it's very dangerous to bring your Queen out early in the play. You might have to trade (lose) her for a weaker piece.

But in the Queen and Pawns Game, you should bring out your Queen early to attack your opponent's Pawns!

	White	Black
6	a4 — a5	Qb4 × b2
7	a5 — a6	Qb2 — b5
8	Qa7 — b7	Qb5 — c5
9	a6 — a7	Qc5 × c2
10	a7 — a8 = Queen!	

(see the diagram at right of the final position of the game)

With his last move, White promoted his Pawn to a Queen! In a full-size game, his opponent is allowed to play on. In the Queen and Pawns Game, the rules say: The first player to move a Pawn safely to the far side of the board is the winner!

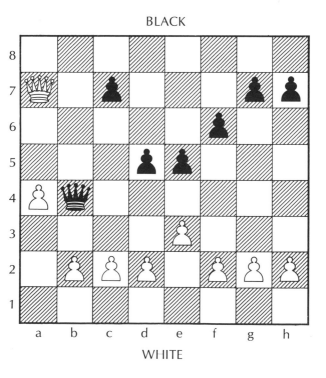

BLACK

WHITE

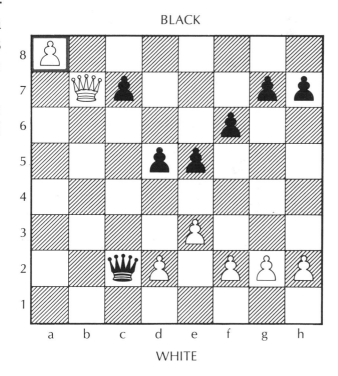

BLACK

WHITE

Now play your own Queen and Pawns Games.

This Is the King

foot soldier. But even the lowly Pawn has a chance to better himself through promotion. The King is a slowpoke throughout the whole game. But without the King there is no game!

In a full-size chess game, and in the King and Pawns Game, each player has one King.

The King rules the chess army. His troops go off to battle, and the King stays in the rear, planning and directing the fight.

The King, compared to his men, has very little fighting power. His officers all move faster. And they travel greater distances in one move than His Highness does. So the officers are expected to do most of the King's fighting for him.

The puny Pawn starts out as a slow-moving

HOW THE KING MOVES

Like the Queen, the King moves in all directions. But his powers are much less than those of the Queen. The King moves over the chessboard on any single play *one square at a time.*

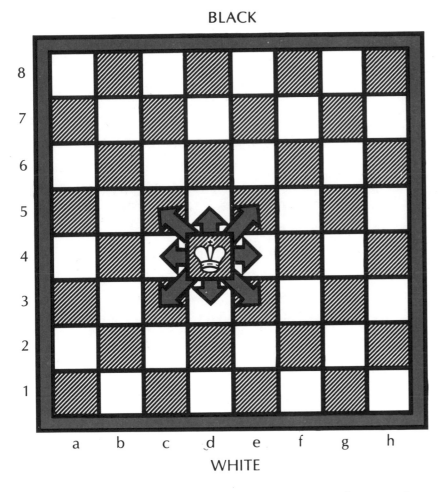

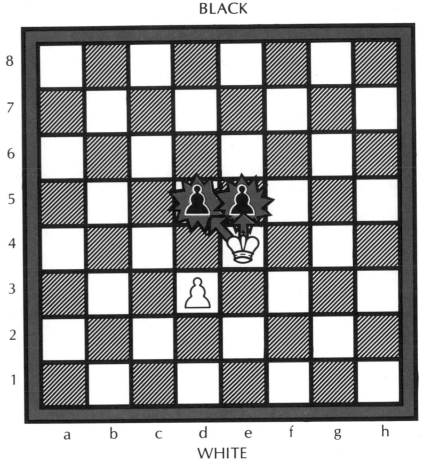

The above picture chessboard shows the King able to move to *any square touching his own square.*

HOW THE KING TAKES ENEMY MEN

The King follows the same rules for taking as all the other chessmen. If an *unprotected enemy piece* is on a square touching the square where the King stands, then the King can take that enemy man.

In the example above, two enemy Pawns stand on squares touching the square where the King stands. In fact, the d5 Pawn has the nerve to attack His Majesty. But happily, both Black Pawns are unprotected. The King can take either one.

71

WHEN THE KING IS LOST, THE GAME IS LOST

In the preceding diagram, the d5 Pawn attacks the White King. A *direct attack* by a man of one army *on the King* of the other army is called **check**. The White King stands directly under the fire of the Black d5 Pawn. White's King is *in check!*

If you want to be extra polite, say "Check" when your piece attacks your opponent's King. The rules of chess do not require it, but for beginners it's better to announce "check" so that there will be less confusion. In the picture chessboard it looks as if the White d3 Pawn protects its King. But this is not so. For a King cannot be traded for any piece at all. *The King in check must escape the check.*

In the picture chessboard, the King in escaping the check can
- (1) move to a square not attacked by an enemy man, *or*
- (2) capture one of the Black Pawns.

Defending against check: When a player's King is in check, the *check must be respected!* A player cannot move another piece until his King *escapes the check.* If a player's King is in check and he accidentally makes a move without defending the check, the player must take back his move and defend the check. His opponent may not capture the King in this case.

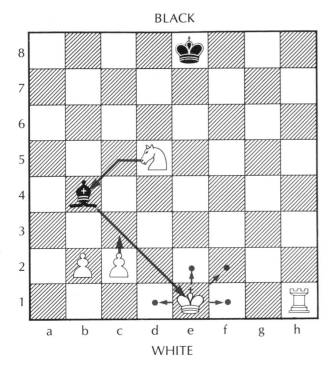

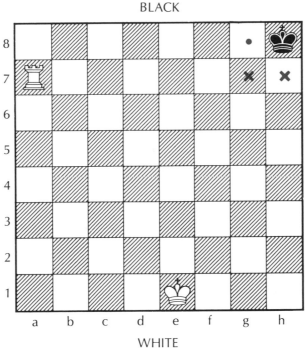

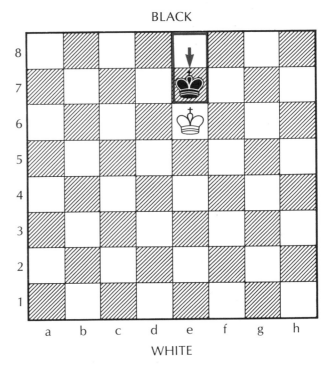

Here the King is in check from Black's Bishop. How does the White player *defend his King against check?*

1. Move the King.

2. *Block* the check. In the picture chessboard, the Pawn move c2 — c3 is a *good block* because the "c" Pawn will be protected by the b2 Pawn.

3. *Take the checking piece.* White's King is not really in trouble. His Knight on *d5* can take the Bishop!

The King may not move into check!

The Rook attacks *g7* and *h7*. So if the King wants to move, he may go only to *g8*.

Kings cannot stand next to each other on touching squares. That's *not allowed* by the rules. A King cannot move into the checking squares of the other King. Kings do not give check to each other, because no King can put himself on a square where he can be taken.

When Kings face each other only one square apart, neither King can move into the other's attack squares (marked "X" in the picture chessboard).

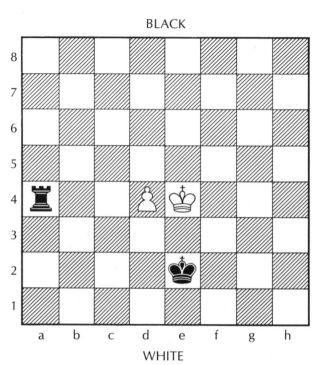

No piece shielding the King may move and thereby expose the King to check. White's King must move off the fourth rank before he can advance his Pawn.

In the diagram, the attacking force of the Black Rook temporarily paralyzes White's Pawn. The Pawn is **pinned** to the White King. The *pin* can be broken either by capturing the Rook (impossible here) or by moving the White King off the Rook's attacking line.

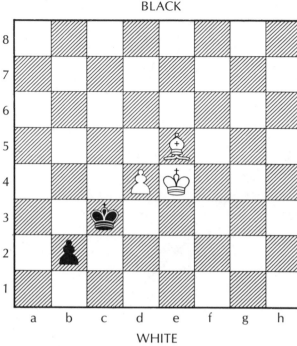

Check may happen indirectly when a piece is moved and the attacking power of another piece is thereby exposed. This is called **discovered check**. In the diagram, White may move his Pawn to d5 so that his *Bishop* checks the Black King. Check is check. *Discovered check* is only a special way of giving check to the King.

When Black moves out of check, White's Bishop takes Black's Pawn to stop its promotion. Then White calmly marches his own Pawn toward the promotion rank.

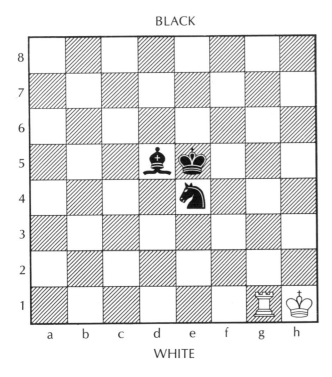

BLACK

WHITE

Discovered double check happens when a King can be put in check from two pieces at the same time. In the diagram, Black's Knight may move to either f2 or g3, giving a Knight check and also exposing the checking power of the Bishop.

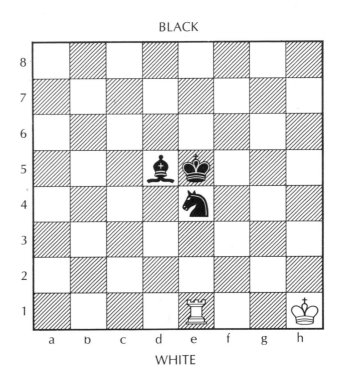

BLACK

WHITE

In this diagram, Black would like to give double check by moving his Knight to f2 or g3. But he is not allowed to expose his own King to check, which he would do if he were to move his Knight immediately. White's Rook *pins* the Knight against the Black King. To move his Knight, Black must either capture White's Rook (impossible here) or move his King off the "e" file to break the pin of the Rook.

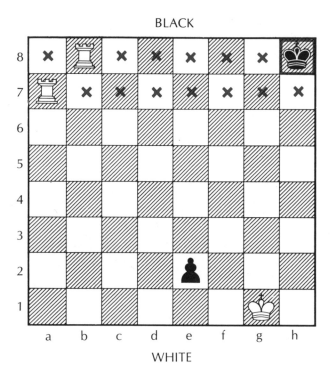

BLACK

WHITE

Checkmate: The player giving checkmate wins the game!

Checkmate happens when the King is in check and the King *cannot escape* from check.

Black's King is in check from the Rook on *b8*. He cannot move up a rank because White's Rook on *a7* covers that line. He also has no piece to put between his King and the b8 Rook to block the check, and no piece with which to capture the Rook. Black loses the game. His King is checkmated!

The Black Pawn would have

saved the day by promoting to a Queen, which could then have given White's King plenty of checks. But White got in checkmate first!

BLACK

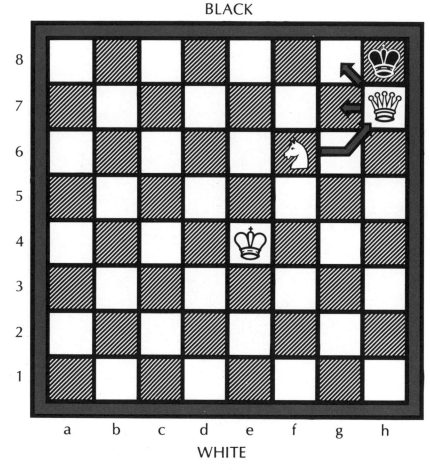

WHITE

The Queen attacks (checks) the Black King and covers all his escape squares. With the help of a protecting Knight, the Queen gives *checkmate* to the Black King. No matter what other pieces may be on the board, *checkmate wins the game!*

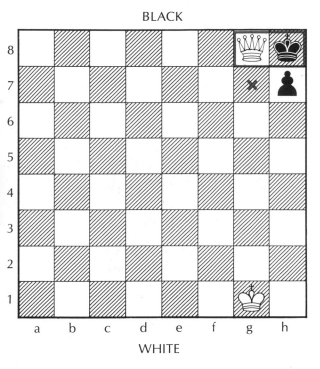

White's Queen completely traps Black's King. The Black King is in check. *But* White's Queen is not protected by a helping piece. Black's King can take the Queen!

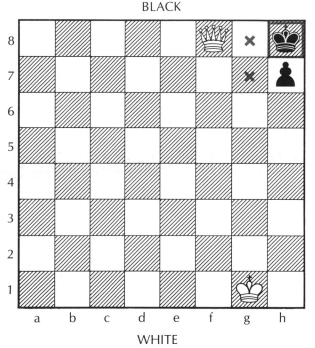

Black's King is checkmated! The King is blocked from escaping by his own Pawn. And White's unprotected Queen is too far away to be taken.

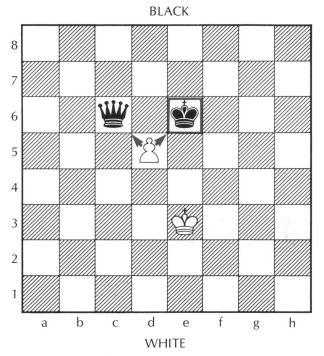

The Pawn checks the King. But the King can take the unprotected Pawn.

The Pawn fork: When a Pawn attacks two enemy pieces at the same time, the situation is called a *Pawn fork*. Here the Pawn checks the King and attacks the Queen.

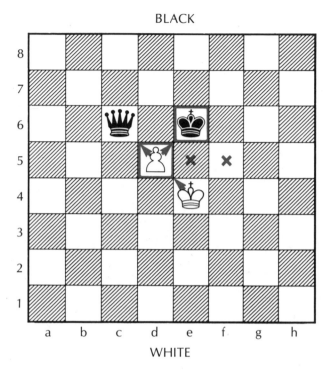

WHITE

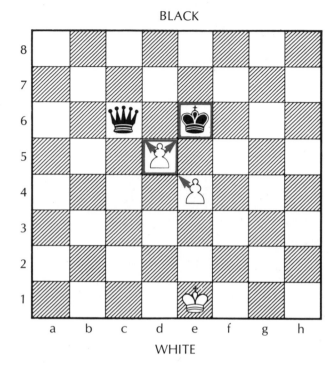

WHITE

The Pawn again *forks* the two most important pieces in the enemy army.

This time White's King protects the Pawn. Black's King *cannot* take the Pawn. But Black's Queen can and must take the Pawn.

The dream fork: The *d5* Pawn forks the King and Queen. The forking Pawn is protected by the Pawn on *e4!*

Black has two choices. (1) He may move his King. Then the d5 Pawn takes the Queen. *Or* (2) the Queen may capture the attacking (checking) Pawn (. . . Qc6 × d5). But then the e4 Pawn takes the Queen (2 e4 × d5) with check! Finally, Black's King can take the last Pawn (2 . . . Ke6 × d5).

SIMPLE SAMPLE CHECKMATES

Here are several simple checkmate situations.

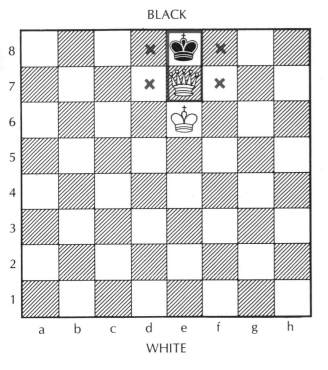

Protected by her King, the Queen checkmates Black's King!

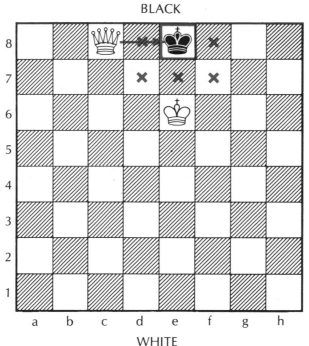

Just as if she were a Rook, the Queen here says, "Checkmate!"

White's King covers escape squares not attacked by the Queen, e7 and f7.

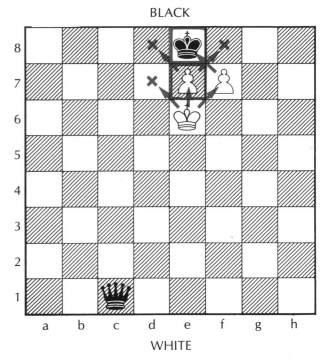

The Black King is trapped by White's King and "e" Pawn. The "f" Pawn gives checkmate!

Black promoted a Pawn and has a Queen. But the Queen could not come to the rescue in time!

See pages 92 to 95 for more examples of check and checkmate situations.

The King and Pawns Game

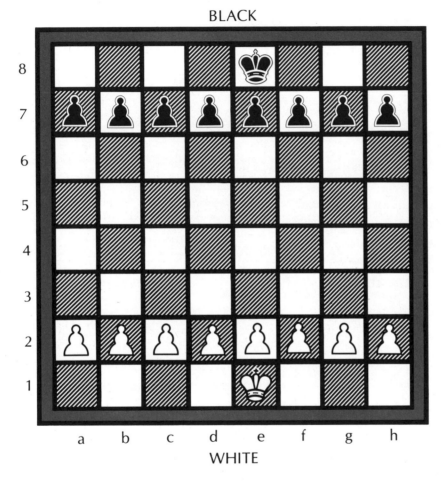

BLACK

WHITE

Knowing so much about the King, you are ready for the King and Pawns Game. Set up the pieces in the positions they would have for a full-size chess game (see above). Note that the Kings begin on squares E1 (White) and E8 (Black).

Now review rules 1 to 4 and 6 to 8 on page 23. Add to these rules the following:

1. Pawns that reach the last rank may be promoted as in the Queen and Pawns Game.

2. The *checking power* of the pieces and the *response of the King to check* are used in this game.

3. *Only* checkmate of the enemy King wins the King and Pawns Game!

Note: For reading a game in algebraic notation, the symbol *K* stands for *King*. There are two symbols used for the word "check":

   (1) + means check to the King, *and*
   (2) *ch* means check to the King. In this book we will use "ch."

Example: *Ke2 — e3* means *the King moves from the e2 square to the e3 square.*

e5 x d4ch means *the Pawn on the e5 square captures an enemy man on the d4 square and gives check to the enemy King.*

Before you play a King and Pawns Game, sharpen your skill by playing over the sample game below on your own chessboard.

	White	*Black*
1	e2 — e4	e7 — e5
2	Ke1 — e2	f7 — f6
3	Ke2 — e3	g7 — g5
4	d2 — d4	e5 × d4ch
5	Ke3 × d4	d7 — d6
6	Kd4 — d5	a7 — a5
7	Kd5 — e6	b7 — b5

(see the diagram)

When you play the full-size chess game, your King will usually move quickly to safety in a corner of the board and remain there until most of the dangerous heavy pieces have gone off the board.

In this King and Pawns Game, however, the White King attacks deep into enemy territory!

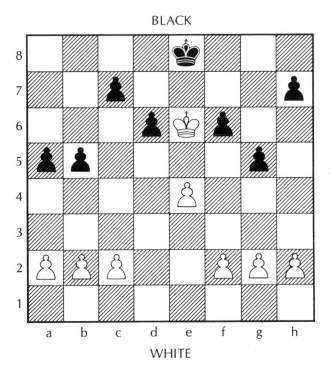

	White	*Black*
8	Ke6 × f6	a5 — a4
9	Kf6 × g5	c7 — c5
10	Kg5 — f6	b5 — b4
11	Kf6 — g7	c5 — c4
12	b2 — b3	a4 × b3
13	a2 × b3	c4 × b3
14	c2 × b3	h7 — h5

(see the diagram)

White has blocked Black's action by a bunch of Pawn trades.

Now White is ready to use his extra Pawns to win the game!

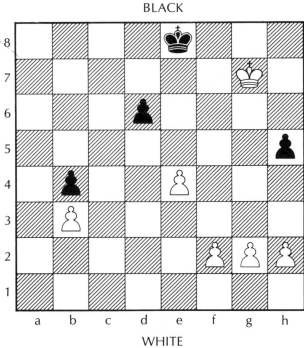

	White	Black
15	f2 — f4	h5 — h4
16	f4 — f5	Ke8 — e7
17	f5 — f6ch	Ke7 — e8
18	f6 — f7ch	Ke8 — e7
19	f7 — f8 = Qch	Ke7 — e6
20	Qf8 — e8 checkmate!	

(see the diagram of the final position of the game)

The Black King cannot escape the Queen's check without moving into the attack squares of the White King or e4 Pawn. Notice that the escape of Black's King is blocked by his own Pawn on d6! Black's King is checkmated. The game is over.

How did White win? The White King captured enough Pawns to clear a path for his own Pawn promotion. The White Queen gave the deadly checkmate very quickly!

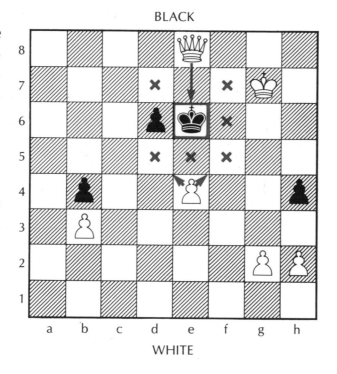

BLACK

WHITE

Now play your own King and Pawns Games.

82

Two Special Moves

You are not ready to play the full-size chess game until you have seen these special moves. After you have seen how they work, you can put them into practice in a full-size game. The more you practice using the special moves in a full-size game, the more you will understand them.

THE SPECIAL MOVE CALLED CASTLING

The battle will rage in the center of the board during a full-size game. To win at chess a player traps his opponent's King. He checkmates the King. If the King moves up to the center early in the game, he will surely be checked and he may be checkmated!

Sitting in the corner, a King has fewer squares to move to. But in the early part of the full-size game, the King is safer in the corner.

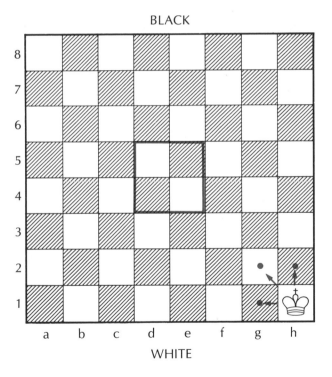

BLACK

WHITE

A long time ago, someone invented a move that quickly carries the King off to the safety of the corner. That move is called **castling**. Castling is the King's power to run to safety. It is a single move of play. In castling, the *King and one of his Rooks* are moved *at the same turn of play*. Castling is the only moment in a chess game when two pieces in the same army are moved in the same turn of play.

square (d1), and the Black Queen always begins battle on a dark square (d8).

One half of the board (the files from "a" to "d") is called the **Queenside**. The other half of the board (the files from "e" to "h") is called the **Kingside**.

A king may castle on the Kingside or on the Queenside. Castling Queenside is called **castling long**, for there are more squares between the King and the Rook on that side. Castling Kingside is called **castling short**. There are fewer squares between the King and the Rook on that side.

BLACK

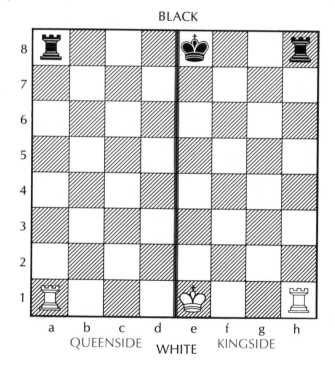

QUEENSIDE WHITE KINGSIDE

With all the other men cleared off the board, this is how the Kings and Rooks stand at the beginning of the full-size chess game.

At the start of all chess games, the White Queen always begins the game on a light

Castling Kingside is usually safer than castling Queenside. Castling Kingside puts the King deeper into a corner of the board. (Compare this illustration with the illustration on page 86.)

CASTLING KINGSIDE

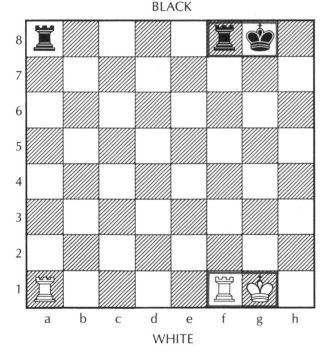

Here you see both sides are castled on the Kingside.

How did this castling happen?

The King moves two squares from his home square toward his Kingside Rook. Then the Kingside Rook is moved from its home square to the square on the other side of the King.

Castling rule one: A King that has already moved from his home square can *never* castle. Even if that King goes back to his home square, he still cannot castle.

85

Castling rule two: If his Kingside Rook has moved from its home square, the King *can never castle Kingside*. Even if the Rook goes back to its home square, the King still cannot castle Kingside!

When your opponent castles Kingside and you castle Queenside, you tell your opponent, "Come and get me!" Each player attacks the other's king on opposite sides of the board.

CASTLING QUEENSIDE

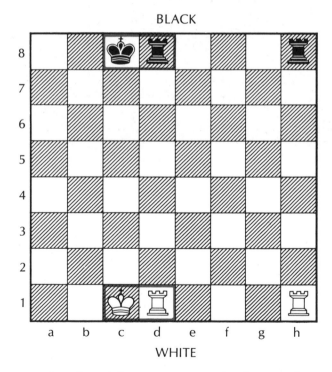

Both sides are castled on the Queenside. How did this happen?

Put the Kings and Rooks on their starting squares on your own chessboard. Then try castling Queenside.

The King moves two squares toward his Queenside Rook. Then the Queenside Rook is moved from its home square to the square on the other side of the King.

Castling rule three: If the Queenside Rook has moved from its home square, the King *can never castle Queenside!* Even if the Rook goes back to its home square, the King still cannot castle Queenside.

Note: If you have no Rook on one side of the board, then your King cannot castle on that side. You need a Castle to castle!

Castling rule four: A King cannot castle if the square where he must land is attacked by an enemy piece. A King cannot move into check!

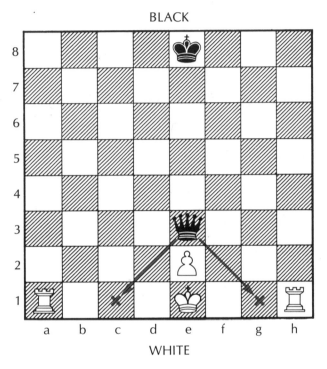

In the picture chessboard above, White cannot castle on either side. Black's Queen attacks both g1 and c1. White may be able to castle later, when the Queen disappears from her attacking position.

Castling rule five: To castle, a King must *pass through* one square before he reaches his final castled position. If that **pass square** is attacked by an enemy piece, the King cannot castle!

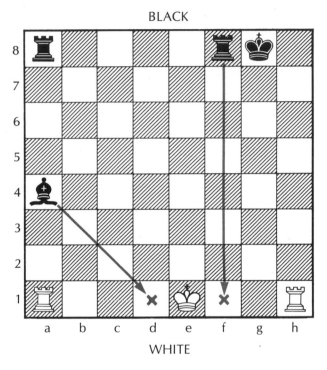

Black's King is already castled. To castle Kingside, White's King must pass through f1. As long as Black's Rook attacks f1, the White King cannot castle short.

To castle Queenside, the White King must pass through d1. As long as Black's Bishop attacks d1, the White King cannot castle long.

Castling rule six: A King in check cannot castle.

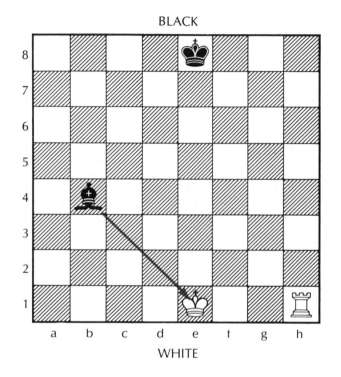

BLACK

WHITE

If the checking piece can be captured or its attack blocked, the checked King can castle later.

If a King is forced to move out of check, that King can never castle!

In the picture chessboard above, the King *must* move out of the attacking fire of the Bishop. That King has lost his castling privilege. He must wait until the next game to castle!

Castling rule seven: A King cannot castle if any piece stands on a square between him and the Rook on the side where he wants to castle.

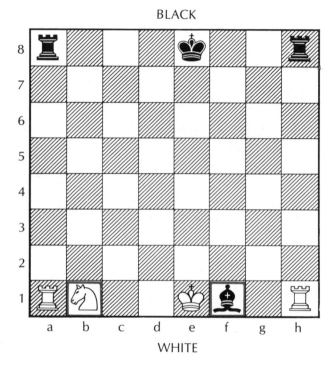

BLACK

WHITE

The Black King in the picture chessboard can castle long or short.

The White King cannot castle Queenside until he moves his Knight out of b1.

On the Kingside, if the White King takes the Bishop, he cannot castle anywhere. If the h1 Rook takes the Bishop, the King can't castle Kingside. Remember, *taking* is a chess move.

If White wants to castle short, some other piece must take the Bishop. In the example the best move is to take the Bishop, even though you lose the right to castle. A piece is a piece! Don't let the enemy Bishop get away!

Finally: A King may still castle even if the Rook he uses is under attack (this can happen with either Rook). A King may also still castle even if the Rook must pass through a square attacked by an enemy piece. This situation can happen only on the Queenside, where the White Rook passes through b1 and the Black Rook passes through b8 (see the diagram below). The point is that White's *King* does not pass through b1, nor does Black's King pass through b8.

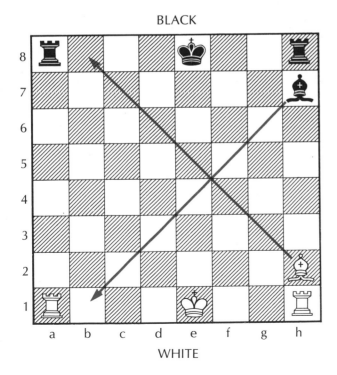

BLACK

WHITE

Note: For writing "castles" in algebraic notation, *castles short* (on the Kingside) is written *0–0*; *castles long* (on the Queenside) is written *0–0–0*.

THE SECOND SPECIAL MOVE IS THE LAST OF THE PAWN POWERS

En passant is a chess term that simply uses two French words that mean *in passing*.

You already know that the Pawn
(1) moves one square forward at one turn of play;
(2) captures on the diagonal;
(3) on its first move has the power to move two squares forward.

Because you know so much about the Pawn, it will be easy to learn the *en passant* move.

En passant gives the Pawn the power to make a very tricky capture!

The true move of any Pawn is one square forward. Moving two squares forward on his first move (from his home square) is a special privilege given the Pawn. The Pawn cannot use the privilege unless he understands that an enemy Pawn still has the right to capture. The capture takes place on the square that the Pawn moving two squares forward *passes through*.

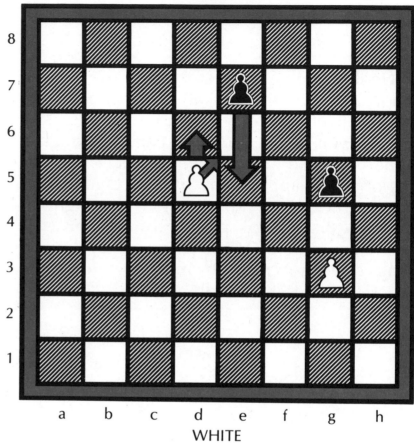

The Black Pawn in the picture chessboard above still stands on his original (home) square. He may move two squares forward. When he does, he *passes* a square attacked by the White Pawn.

The White Pawn may simply move forward, or not move at all. He does not have to take *en passant*. But if he does take *en passant*, he must do it *on the very next turn of play*.

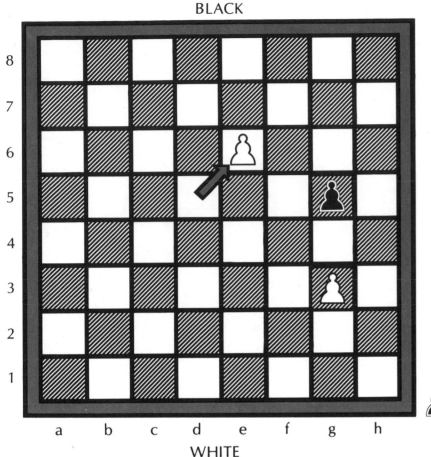

BLACK

8 7 6 5 4 3 2 1

a b c d e f g h

WHITE

In the diagram, Black's Pawn has landed on e5. In taking *en passant,* the player with White takes the Black Pawn off the board. He then puts his own "d" Pawn on e6. The *en passant* capture happens just as if the Black Pawn had moved only to e6 instead of to e5.

In algebraic notation the *en passant* capture in the picture chessboard is written *d5 X e5 e.p.* But the taking piece lands not on e5 but on e6!

Black moved his Pawn from e7 to e5. The White "d" Pawn has taken *en passant.* How did this happen?

In every other case, when a chess piece takes an enemy piece, the taking piece lands on the square left open by the captured piece. This does not happen with *en passant.* In *en passant,* the capturing Pawn lands on the square *where the enemy Pawn would have been if he had made his one-square-forward move.*

Check and Checkmate

Since the object of a game is to achieve checkmate, here are some examples of check and checkmate positions.

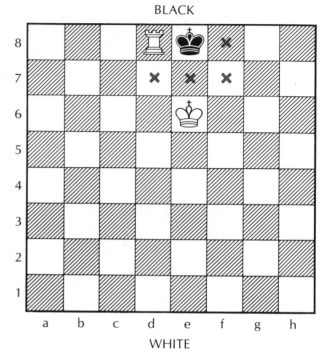

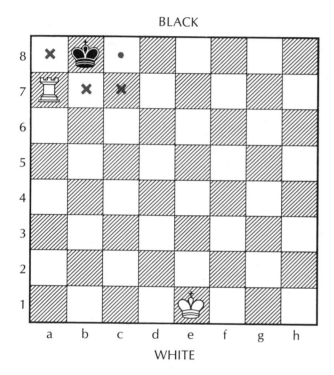

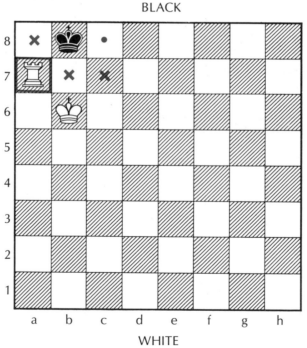

The Rook covers three squares marked in the picture chess-board, besides covering the whole of rank 7.

But if it is Black's move, his King can take the Rook!

Black's King can move only to *c8*. White's Rook is protected by his King.

Black's King has no choice. He must take White's Rook. Check must be defended!

BLACK

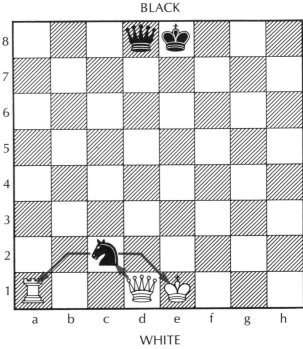

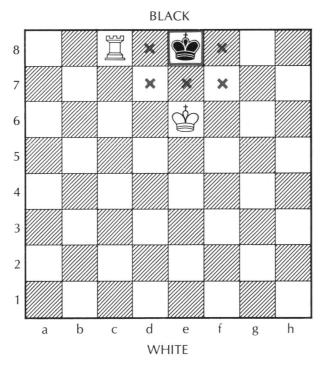

White's Rook is protected by the Bishop. Black's King is checkmated!

The Black King is checkmated! White's Rook is too far away to be captured!

The *fork* is also the Knight's secret weapon!

The Black Knight checks the White King and attacks the Rook at the same time. The Knight is *forking* King and Rook!

The Knight's check *can never be blocked!*

If the White King moves away from the check, the Knight can take the Rook.

In this example, however, White's Queen can safely capture the Knight. There is no piece protecting the lone Horse!

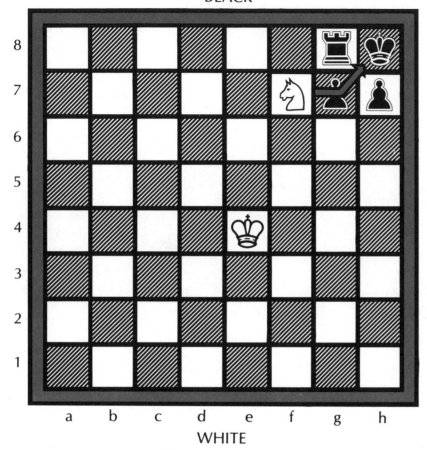

BLACK

WHITE

The Knight cannot be captured!

Checked by the Knight, the Black King cannot move. He cannot escape the check by taking his own men and is sadly locked in the corner by them. The Knight has checkmated Black's King smothered in his castle!

The Knight's check cannot be blocked. So Black has lost. The Knight has given "smothered mate"!

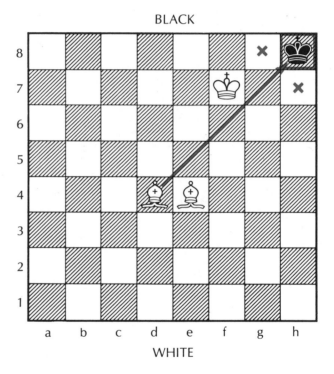

BLACK

WHITE

The dark-squared Bishop gives check to the King!

The light-squared Bishop covers the escape square h7. And the White King cuts off the space at g8.

It is checkmate!

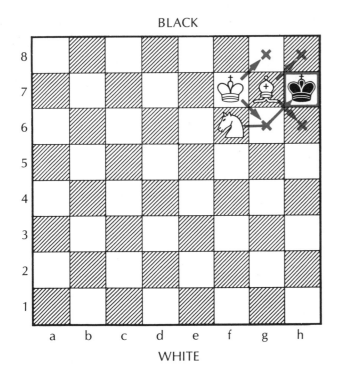

BLACK

WHITE

The White King and Bishop surround the Black King.

The Knight deals the knockout punch — checkmate!

How many pieces does a player need to force checkmate against a lone King?

To force checkmate, a player needs at least one Pawn — for a Pawn can be promoted to a Queen or a Rook. And *Queen with King* or *Rook with King* can *always force checkmate against the lone enemy King*. If you have the lone King, hope for *stalemate!* When you are trying for checkmate, watch out for stalemate!

You should know that *King and Bishop, King and Knight,* and even *King and two Knights cannot force checkmate against a lone King.*

When you have only one more piece than your opponent, be careful not to trade off all your Pawns!

Stalemate

When a player has no legal move, *but is not in check,* he is in *stalemate.* You are already familiar with stalemate situations in the Pawns Games (page 24).

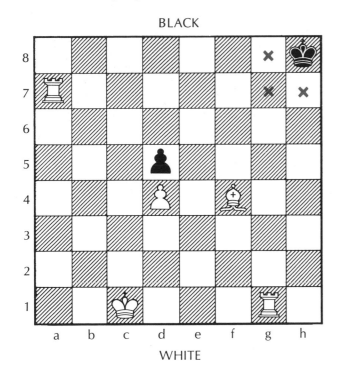

BLACK

WHITE

In the diagram above, Black's Pawn is blocked. His King is boxed in by the White Rooks. Black cannot move his Pawn. And he is not allowed to move his King into check. Black is not in check, but he has no legal move. So if it is Black's move, he is stalemated. The game is a draw. If it is White's move, he may checkmate with Bf4 — e5.

When a player is ahead by one piece or many pieces, he does not want a draw unless there is some special danger present. If it is White's move in the picture chessboard, he should *release the stalemate,* since checkmate is not immediately possible. He could do this either by moving one Rook away from rank 7 or by moving the other Rook off the ''g'' file.

If you want to checkmate your opponent's King, be sure your opponent on the move always has room for one move as you prepare to give checkmate or lead him into the mating net. After you checkmate your opponent's King, there will be no moves to worry about!

The following picture chessboards show the Black King stalemated by different White chessmen. Black is on move and he has no legal move. The game is a draw. (You may put White pieces where the Black pieces stand, and Black pieces where the White pieces stand. It comes to the same thing: White will be on move, and White will be stalemated.)

In the examples below, the stronger side would win if he were on move! Most stalemates happen because the player with the advantage is careless.

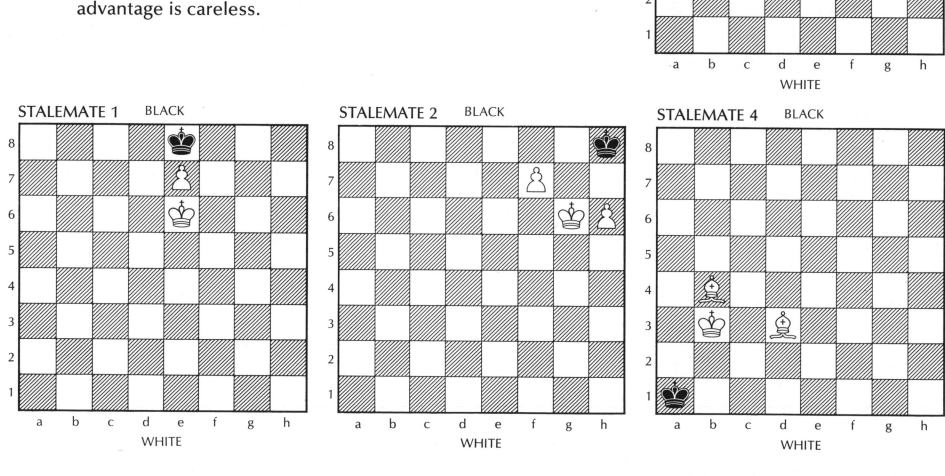

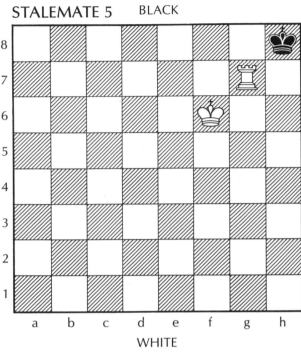

STALEMATE 5

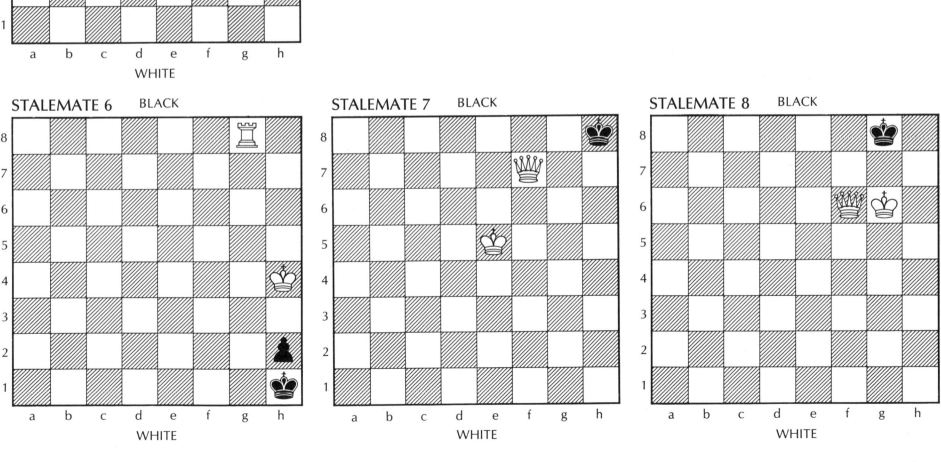

STALEMATE 6

STALEMATE 7

STALEMATE 8

The Point-Count Value of the Chessmen

the Queen — the all-powerful! — 9 points

the Rook — second most
powerful! — 5 points

the Bishop — a bit better than a
Knight! — 3 points

the Knight — the tricky hopping
Horse! — 3 points

the Pawn — the weakest but
full of surprises! — 1 point

the King — he has no point
value! — 0 points

If your King gets checkmated, you lose the game. This is true even if you have on the board many more pieces than your opponent! *Knowing the value of the pieces is very important!*

Suppose you want to take an opponent's piece with one of your pieces? Suppose also that your opponent can take the piece that took his piece. One side capturing and then the other side capturing is a *trade*. A player gives one piece in return for another. Before you make a move to trade pieces, figure the value of the piece you're giving (your taking piece) against the value of the piece you're getting (the piece you want to capture). Using the point-count value of the chessmen is a good idea!

Now you are ready to play a game of chess with all the pieces!

The Chess Armies Before a Full-Size Fighting Game

Now that you've mastered all the Pawns Games and have learned about castling, capturing *en passant*, checkmate, and stalemate, you can start to master the full-size game.

Set up your own pieces on a chessboard as in the picture below.

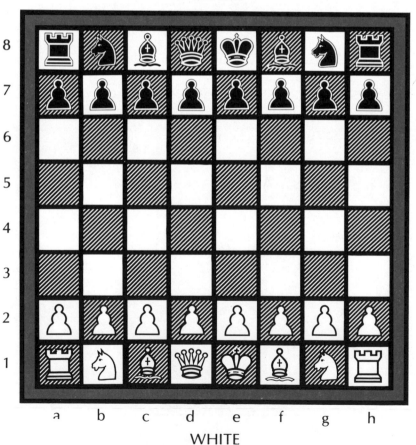

BLACK

WHITE

Before you play your first big chess game with a friend, play over the practice games below on your own chessboard.

GAME 1

White	Black
1 f2 — f4	e7 — e6
2 g2 — g4	Qd8 — h4

The Fool's Checkmate!

GAME 2

White	Black
1 d2 — d4	Ng8 — f6
2 Nb1 — d2	e7 — e5
3 d4 × e5	Nf6 — g4
4 h2 — h3	Ng4 — e3
5 f2 × e3	Qd8 — h4ch
6 g2 — g3	Qh4 × g3

A Dunce's Checkmate!

GAME 3

White	Black
1 e2 — e4	e7 — e5
2 Bf1 — c4	Bf8 — c5
3 Qd1 — h5	Ng8 — f6
4 Qh5 × f7	

The Scholar's Checkmate!

GAME 4

White	Black
1 e2 — e4	e7 — e5
2 f2 — f4	Bf8 — c5
3 f4 × e5	Qd8 — h4ch
4 Ke1 — e2	Qh4 × e4

Checkmate in the center!

GAME 5

White	Black
1 e2 — e4	e7 — e5
2 Ng1 — f3	d7 — d6
3 Bf1 — c4	h7 — h6
4 Nb1 — c3	Bc8 — g4
5 Nf3 × e5	Bg4 × d1
6 Bc4 × f7ch	Ke8 — e7
7 Nc3 — d5	

Checkmate in a crowd!

GAME 6

White	Black
1 e2 — e4	e7 — e5
2 Ng1 — f3	Nb8 — c6
3 Bf1 — c4	Nc6 — d4
4 Nf3 × e5	Qd8 — g5
5 Ne5 × f7	Qg5 × g2
6 Rh1 — f1	Qg2 × e4ch
7 Bc4 — e2	Nd4 — f3

A Smothered Checkmate!

Descriptive Chess Notation

There is another way for reading and writing chess moves. You have seen algebraic notation. Now you will see **descriptive notation**. Learning descriptive notation is a little bit harder. But as you progress as a chess player, it's important to know descriptive notation because many books and chess magazines still use descriptive notation. And many books written a long time ago have the games of the great masters. You'll want to be able to read the games in all those books and magazines!*

The symbols for the pieces are the same in descriptive notation as in algebraic notation!

K is for *King*
Q is for *Queen*
R is for *Rook*
B is for *Bishop*
N (or sometimes *Kt*) is for *Knight*

In algebraic notation, a Pawn move is written simply by naming the square where the Pawn stands and the square to which it is going.

P is for *Pawn* in descriptive notation.

*Note for adults on descriptive notation: It is more important for the child to have fun playing chess than to struggle excessively over learning descriptive notation! After the child has played chess for a few months and shows interest in playing over games from other books, magazines, and newspaper columns, you can help the child learn descriptive notation.

All the other symbols mean the same thing in both notations!

The dash (—) is for *to* (some square).
× is for *takes* (an enemy piece).
The letters *e.p.* tell you a Pawn is taking *en passant*.
+ or *ch* means *check* to the King.
0–0 tells you a King *castles on the Kingside*.
0–0–0 tells you a King *castles on the Queenside*.

THE CHESSBOARD IN DESCRIPTIVE NOTATION

The chessboard is divided in half. The file where the Queens stand and the files to White's left are called the Queenside. The file where the Kings stand and the files to White's right are called the Kingside.

Each file has a name. A file is named after the chess officer stationed on that file as a game begins.

The Kings stand on the *King File*. The Kings have helpers. A *King's Bishop* stands on the *King's Bishop File*. A *King's Knight* stands on the *King's Knight File*. And the *King's Rook* stands on the *King's Rook File*.

The Queens stand on the *Queen File*. The Queens have helpers. The *Queen's Bishop* stands on the *Queen's Bishop File*. The *Queen's Knight* stands on the *Queen's Knight File*. And the *Queen's Rook* stands on the *Queen's Rook File*.

The Pawns standing on each file from left to right in the picture chessboard below are named for the chessmen stationed on each file (*Queen's Rook Pawn, Queen's Knight Pawn,* and so on).

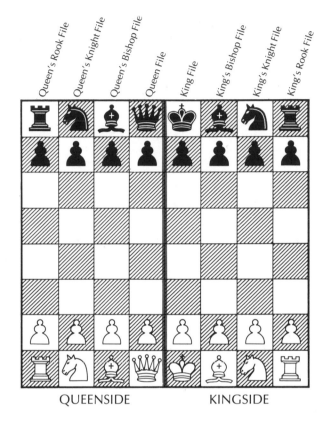

In descriptive notation, each square has two names, one name from White's side of the board, and another name from Black's side of the board.

The ranks are numbered from 1 to 8 from White's side of the board. And again the ranks are numbered from 1 to 8 from Black's side of the board.

The squares take their names from the name of the file and the number of the rank where they stand.

BLACK

8	QR8	QN8	QB8	Q8	K8	KB8	KN8	KR8
7	QR7	QN7	QB7	Q7	K7	KB7	KN7	KR7
6	QR6	QN6	QB6	Q6	K6	KB6	KN6	KR6
5	QR5	QN5	QB5	Q5	K5	KB5	KN5	KR5
4	QR4	QN4	QB4	Q4	K4	KB4	KN4	KR4
3	QR3	QN3	QB3	Q3	K3	KB3	KN3	KR3
2	QR2	QN2	QB2	Q2	K2	KB2	KN2	KR2
1	QR1	QN1	QB1	Q1	K1	KB1	KN1	KR1

WHITE

Here you see the squares named and the ranks numbered from White's side. Check for the names of the files in the picture chessboard on page 103.

Suppose you want to find White's *Queen's Rook 6 (QR6)* square? Put your finger on rank 6 and move it over to the Queen's Rook File.

What about *King's Bishop 4 (KB4)* square? Put your finger on rank 4 and move it over to the King's Bishop File.

Now you walk around to the other side of the board to see the names of the squares from Black's side.

WHITE

8	KR8	KN8	KB8	K8	Q8	QB8	QN8	QR8
7	KR7	KN7	KB7	K7	Q7	QB7	QN7	QR7
6	KR6	KN6	KB6	K6	Q6	QB6	QN6	QR6
5	KR5	KN5	KB5	K5	Q5	QB5	QN5	QR5
4	KR4	KN4	KB4	K4	Q4	QB4	QN4	QR4
3	KR3	KN3	KB3	K3	Q3	QB3	QN3	QR3
2	KR2	KN2	KB2	K2	Q2	QB2	QN2	QR2
1	KR1	KN1	KB1	K1	Q1	QB1	QN1	QR1

BLACK

When you looked at the board from White's side, you found the White King on your right and the White Queen on your left. Look from Black's side. The Black King is on your left. And the Black Queen is on your right. But the names for the files stay the same!

Find Black's *King 4* square. His *Queen 7* square. His *King's Knight 6* square. Try to name some of the squares yourself. Try both from White's side and from Black's side of the board.

A CHESS GAME WRITTEN IN DESCRIPTIVE NOTATION

In algebraic notation a square has only one name. In descriptive notation you'll have to look for two names for each square. But that's not really so hard. Just keep your eyes open!

A move in descriptive notation first names the piece moving and then names the square to which the piece is going.

P — K4 means *a Pawn moves to the fourth square on the King File.* If Black plays *P — K4,* that's the same Pawn move from his side of the board.

A capture names the piece taking and the piece being taken. *Queen takes Queen* is written *Q x Q.*

Here are some games written in descriptive notation. If you compare them with the practice games on page 101, you will discover that they are the same! See if you can play over these games on your own chessboard from the descriptive notations below.

If you want more practice in reading descriptive notation, get a book that has a collection of short games. Play over the games on your own chessboard.

GAME 1

	White	Black
1	P — KB4	P — K3
2	P — KN4	Q — R5

The Fools' Checkmate!

GAME 2

	White	Black
1	P — Q4	N — KB3
2	N — Q2	P — K4
3	P × P	N — N5
4	P — KR3	N — K6
5	P × N	Q — R5ch
6	P — N3	Q × P

A Dunce's Checkmate!

GAME 3

	White	Black
1	P — K4	P — K4
2	B — B4	B — B4
3	Q — R5	N — KB3
4	Q × Pch-mate	

The Scholar's Checkmate!

GAME 4

	White	Black
1	P — K4	P — K4
2	P — KB4	B — B4
3	P × P	Q — R5ch
4	K — K2	Q × Pch-mate

Checkmate in the center!

GAME 5

	White	Black
1	P — K4	P — K4
2	N — KB3	P — Q3
3	B — B4	P — KR3
4	N — B3	B — N5
5	N × P	B × Q
6	B × Pch	K — K2
7	N — Q5ch-mate	

Checkmate in a crowd!

GAME 6

White	Black
P — K4	P — K4
N — KB3	N — QB3
B — B4	N — Q5
N × P	Q — N4
N × BP	Q × P
R — B1	Q × KPch
B — K2	N — B6ch-mate

A Smothered Checkmate!

Now play chess, and play it for fun!

Index of Terms